Start Your Own

FREELANCE WRITING BUSINESS AND MORE

Additional titles in *Entrepreneur's* **Startup Series**

Start Your Own

Entrepreneur
MAGAZINE'S

startup

Start Your Own

FREELANCE WRITING BUSINESS AND MORE

Copywriter • Proofreader Copy Editor • Journalist

Entrepreneur Press and George Sheldon

EP
Entrepreneur
Press

Jere L. Calmes, Publisher
Managing Editor: Marla Markman
Cover Design: Beth Hansen-Winter
Production and Composition: Eliot House Productions

This publication is designed to provide accurate and authoritative information in regard
to the subject matter covered. It is sold with the understanding that the publisher is not
engaged in rendering legal, accounting or other professional services. If legal advice or
other expert assistance is required, the services of a competent professional person
should be sought.

Library of Congress Cataloging-in-Publication Data

Sheldon, George.
  Start your own freelance writing business and more/by Entrepreneur Press and George
Sheldon.
      p.   cm.
  ISBN-13: 978-1-59918-175-2 (alk. paper)
  ISBN-10: 1-59918-175-4 (alk. paper)
      1. Advertising copy. 2. Small business—Management. I. Entrepreneur Press. II.
Title.
HF5825.S48 2008
659.13'20681—dc22   2007026691

Printed in Canada

13 12 11 10 09 08   10 9 8 7 6 5 4 3 2 1

Contents

Preface

Are you looking for a homebased business that uses your creativity and your willingness to work, offers low overhead, is easy to start, and can be quite lucrative? Welcome to freelance writing. This is a business that offers the opportunity to make more than $100,000 each year. And there is always room for one more writer.

Of course, the public perception is that you earn only a meager wage while working in excess of 100 hours a week. Eccentric and craggy, you are seen as a starving artist. Your friends and family probably think you survive by eating cat food, always leaving each can half full so as to feed your scrawny feline as you try to cobble together another manuscript. You probably have little (if any) heat in the winter. They certainly think you are doomed to be a pauper, but you are doing what you want to do. It's an image helped by many movies and television shows.

In reality, operating a writing business is quite different. You often have the freedom to work the hours you want to work. Your lifestyle, based on income, can be quite good. What determines your income is how well you manage your writing business and how well you manage your time. Within these pages is all the practical advice you need to launch your freelance writing business. You'll be amazed at how easy it is to get started and how soon you can earn money.

The information here gives you the insider's view of the business. You'll learn how to get started, where to find work, what to do, and just as importantly, what not to do. You are going to learn how to establish an internet presence, how to develop a client list, and what you need to get started. You are also going to learn how to expand your freelance writing business in other directions so you can earn more by offering services and informational products.

Freelance Writing
Today and Tomorrow

Imagine opening a business that takes very little money to start. You can work in your pajamas, if you want. You do most, if not all, of your work from your own home. You choose your work hours.

Welcome to the world of freelance writing! Here is a business opportunity that offers all of the above, plus many other benefits. You operate your own business, choose assignments, get your work done, and collect your fees. The trip to the bank always makes you smile.

The world of freelance writing is wide, competitive, and open. One of its benefits is the ease of getting started. No matter in what area you choose to work, you can quickly offer your services as a freelancer.

In many businesses it takes weeks or months (if not a year or more) of planning before you can start your enterprise. It doesn't work that way in freelancing. Getting started as a freelancer in most fields, including writing, is fast and easy. You can literally start this morning and be earning income this afternoon. Freelancing is often associated with journalism and the publishing industry because writers, editors, graphic artists, and photographers often work as freelancers. Because it's popular in many areas, consultants, coaches, and mentors often work as freelancers. Many computer programmers, database developers, and application consultants work as freelancers. So you'll never be alone.

By using the internet to communicate, freelancer writers have extended their services and can seek assignments worldwide. Freelancing today often involves working with clients who are not located nearby. And even when the client is close-at-hand, e-mail and phone calls are still usually the means of communication between client and freelancer.

Freelancers are often confused with independent or temporary workers. Independent workers are not employees, but they are often bound to one company or client. Freelancers seek work and assignments from various clients. This is what makes a freelancer unique. The freelancer works until a project is complete and moves on, looking for another assignment from another client or source. Many freelance writers, however, do have enduring relationships with some clients.

A freelancer is simply a worker pursuing a profession without a formal commitment to, or employment contract with, any one person or entity. Freelancers develop clients and contacts, and work on projects as needed. Typical freelancers are fiercely independent, choosing to do the project work or assignments during their chosen hours. All freelancers work on a deadline, a predefined time when the work must be completed and turned in to the client. The freelancer is then paid for the work completed. Among those offering freelance writing services, there are part-timers making a few extra dollars, full-timers making a decent living, and sought-after professionals commanding high fees.

Fun Fact

The term "free-lancer" was first used by Sir Walter Scott (1771–1832) in his well-known historical romance *Ivanhoe* to describe a "medieval mercenary warrior."

> **Tip...**
>
> **Smart Tip**
>
> Many freelancers leave regular employment and enter freelancing to "work for myself." Freelancing requires that you work for a client. Your client is your boss. Freelancers soon learn one important fact: they are not "working for myself."

Many freelancing assignments include a degree of creativity. While some assignments require exacting work, often freelancers add their own creative inspirations to the finished product. A writer uses words to develop an interesting magazine article. A photographer uses an artistic eye to produce images that convey a message through the photograph. Programmers often use special tricks to make their computer applications easier to use.

Self-employment offers great autonomy, freedom of expression, and flexible scheduling. This is what attracts freelancers to the freelancing lifestyle. However, income can fluctuate and be uncertain at times. The continuous, time-consuming search for new clients can also be stressful.

Earning Potential

Freelancing offers journalists, authors, and writers an excellent earning potential. Yet, many freelancers do not earn as much as they could because they operate their writing businesses poorly. They do not properly market their services or expertise. They fail to seek more lucrative opportunities and overlook obvious assignments that could enhance their income. Freelance writers who properly operate their writing businesses, market themselves as experts, and seek new opportunities can earn more than $100,000 per year.

According to the Bureau of Labor Statistics, there are vast opportunities for writers, editors, and others working in print media. From reporters to journalists, technical writers to editors, the medium salary ranges from $40K to $75K for those employed by companies and organizations. There is more good news from the Bureau of Labor Statistics. It reports that "Employment of writers and editors is expected to grow about as fast as the average for all occupations through the year 2014."

The overall outlook for most writing and editing jobs is also expected to be competitive because many people with writing or journalism training are attracted to the field. On the surface, this may sound discouraging. But there are

Stat Fact

The Bureau of Labor Statistics expects additional opportunities from expansions and as those currently employed move into other professions or retire.

plenty of opportunities now, and there will be in the future, too. The Bureau of Labor Statistics projects that:

> *Employment of salaried writers and editors for newspapers, periodicals, book publishers, and nonprofit organizations is expected to increase as demand grows for these publications. Magazines and other periodicals increasingly are developing market niches, appealing to readers with special interests. Businesses and organizations are developing newsletters and web sites, and more companies are experimenting with publishing materials directly on the internet. Online publications and services are growing in number and sophistication, spurring the demand for writers and editors, especially those with web experience. Advertising and public relations agencies, which also are growing, should be another source of new jobs.*

This Bureau of Labor Statistics information does not include the self-employed, as most freelancers are. There is, in fact, no single source of statistical information about freelancing. Many people enter freelancing as a part-time or temporary endeavor, only to leave when a full-time job opening is located. The job outlook, however, suggests many new opportunities for freelancers.

The Bureau also predicts that there should be many prospects for

> *technical writers and those with training in a specialized field. Demand for technical writers and writers with expertise in areas such as law, medicine, or economics is expected to increase because of the continuing expansion of scientific and technical information and the need to communicate it to others. Legal, scientific, and technological developments and discoveries generate demand for people to interpret technical information for a more general audience. Rapid growth and change in the high-technology and electronics industries result in a greater need for people to write users' guides, instruction manuals, and training materials. This work requires people who not only are technically skilled as writers, but also are familiar with the subject area.*

Kinds of Freelancing

Are you looking to fill some free time? Do you want to earn extra money? Some freelancers work only to supplement their income. They pursue small, part-time jobs that produce nominal income.

Are you planning to be a full-time freelancer? Is your goal to be self-employed? Do you want to maximize your income and take on exciting assignments? Many freelancers do just that. They work at building a long-term professional practice, one that is capable of producing ongoing and significant income for years.

The Many Titles of Nonfiction Writers

Nonfiction writers are called many things. Because of writing specialties, the titles can get specific. Some the titles assigned to writers are:

- ❍ Copywriter
- ❍ Sportswriter
- ❍ Journalist
- ❍ Travel writer
- ❍ Outdoors writer
- ❍ Medical writer
- ❍ Correspondent
- ❍ Stringer
- ❍ Columnist

The variety of titles holds true in many areas of freelancing, which may be why there are not many readily available statistics about freelancing. Because freelancers can adopt many different titles, it is not easy to keep track of them.

Most freelancers work alone, but employ other freelancers when needed. For example, photographers who accept wedding assignments often engage a second photographer. The second photographer is hired for a few hours to cover a limited assignment. Writers sometimes employ copyeditors to finetune books or articles before they submit the finished work. Keep in mind that you might want to work as a freelancer who assists other freelancers. By doing this, finding work is usually easier.

Bright Idea

While your schedule is up to you to set, you are often at the mercy of others. Use an appointment book to set up interviews, meetings, and phone calls. The better you can master scheduling your time and your work, the more successful you can be as a freelancer.

The Market for Freelancers

There are various reasons why a client engages a freelancer. They include:

- *A project is temporary*. The client only needs additional work done for a specific period of time. For example, a new products directory is being published.

- *Specific expertise is required.* The client needs precise knowledge as part of a project or task. The client—or the client's staff—does not have that expertise, and needs it to complete the project. An example might be writing copy for a computer company's web site.

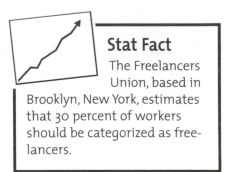

Stat Fact
The Freelancers Union, based in Brooklyn, New York, estimates that 30 percent of workers should be categorized as freelancers.

- *Specific equipment is not available.* The freelancer often uses his or her own equipment and does not require anything from the client. For example, a copyeditor might have an indexing program that a client needs—but only for one project.

- *Adding an employee does not make economical sense.* While a client could employ another person, to do so takes time. It is also expensive to search, interview, investigate, and employ an additional worker.

- *There is no additional overhead expense.* Most freelance assignments do not require the client to provide office space or other items that increase overhead because most assignments do not need to be completed at the client's location.

- *The work needs to be done now.* Current work load at the client's office is such that additional projects cannot be assigned the current staff. The only way to get the work done is to assign it to a temporary worker or freelancer.

There can be other reasons a client wants the services of a freelancer, but they usually boil down to either time or money. It is often cheaper to make an assignment to a freelancer, pay for the work, and move on to the next thing that needs to be done.

Accepting Rejection

A writer who is not receiving many rejections is most probably not working hard. Rejections mean you are working and seeking opportunities. If you are not getting rejected, you are not pitching enough ideas.

You must learn to accept rejection. A big part of any editor's job is to say no. Your ideas or work can be rejected for any number of reasons. It is not always that you have created something terrible (although that could be the reason). Your idea could be rejected because the editor just bought a similar piece. Your editor could be out of money and cannot afford to buy your work. The editor is in a bad mood. These are all things that you cannot control. Expect rejections. It is part of the nonfiction writer's life.

Often, work needs to be done by a specific date, and to get it done on time, additional assistance is required. Sometimes, the work needs to be done over weekends or holidays, and regular staff doesn't want to do it. Regularly scheduled vacations for the client's staff are another reason why a freelancer may be needed.

In addition, employees are expensive. It costs more than ever to cover their benefits. Hospitalization insurance is expensive. Employment taxes are costly. By using a freelancer, the client avoids these ever-expanding costs.

Beware!
Just because the client is not paying for the typical employment costs that go beyond salary, do not overlook your need to pay the premiums for medical insurance, self-employment taxes, and other standard benefits. Make sure your fees cover these expenses.

2

The Freelancing World

Running the Business

Working as a freelancer offers unbeliev-
able freedom. Your independence often means working hours
that you want to work. It also includes the ability to work in
sweats or shorts. You can take as many breaks as you want. Your
office is usually in your home. You don't have to start working

until 2 P.M., or you can start early and quit early to enjoy golf or some other outdoor activity.

Of course, it's still up to you to get the work completed. Many freelancers burn the midnight oil to get a pressing assignment done before an 8 A.M. deadline. If your assignment is to write a magazine article, or label and stuff envelopes, or design a logo, it doesn't matter when the work gets done. It could be started at 6 A.M. or 6 P.M. That's one of the great freedoms of being a freelancer.

Life as a Freelancer

The great benefit of freelancing is flexibility. Clients don't care how the work gets done—they just want it completed on time, on budget, and correctly. Beyond that, they don't care. And freelancers generally take advantage of this freedom. They wear what they want while working. They retreat to their kitchens for comfort-food snacks or lunches. They reward themselves with specialty drinks that lurk in their pantries.

They also have the opportunity to goof off. Instead of working, they can divert their attention to television, the backyard, shopping, household chores, or any other activity that needs attention. It's easy to not work. "Doing it later" can and does occur. As a freelancer, however, it is important to develop a schedule, and stick to it.

As a working freelancer, you must establish a work schedule, and then get into your office and work. The importance of the work schedule remains whether you have an assignment or not. You get to choose those hours. Set it up, and stick with it.

One New Jersey freelancer starts her workday at 10 A.M. At noon, she stops working. She takes a two-and-a-half-hour lunch break during which she runs errands, meets friends for lunch, or completes household chores. On sunny days

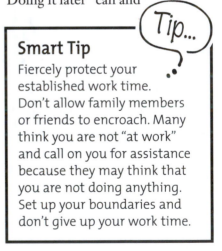

Smart Tip

Fiercely protect your established work time. Don't allow family members or friends to encroach. Many think you are not "at work" and call on you for assistance because they may think that you are not doing anything. Set up your boundaries and don't give up your work time.

in the summer, a backyard nap while sunbathing builds her tan. Precisely at 2:30 P.M., she is back at her desk and works until 6 P.M. Her door is closed, and she works on assignments. Following dinner, she returns to work for several more hours, and depending on the work load, puts in the hours necessary to get her work completed.

Other freelancers have different schedules. Some start their days early, getting up and beginning work between 7 and 8 A.M. They are at their desks and keep working through the day until 4 or 5 P.M. It is almost duplicative of a typical office job. The only difference is they control their time away from their desks.

Many freelancers work through lunch breaks or skip them altogether. Others stop and enjoy the downtime, perhaps catching the latest news on television or taking an extended break that includes some form of exercise.

The important thing for you is to develop a steady work schedule—one that is regular and routine—and stick to it. It doesn't matter what works for you. It is just a matter of establishing a schedule. Because freelancers often have "free time" in their work schedules, they can be diverted. This is particularly true when waiting for a client. Often work is expected but has not arrived. Rather than try to find another working assignment, the freelancer blows off the schedule. This is a mistake. Keep to your schedule.

Just as a "boss" would not allow you to goof off for hours (or days) at a job, you should not slack off either. Planning your schedule is vitally important. There is always something to do. Use your downtime properly to maximize your freelance business.

Setting Up a Schedule

Plan your workweeks. Whether you use a computer to track your daily activities, a simple calendar, or a daily planner, keep track of your appointments. Schedule routine appointments during those times when you are not scheduling work.

Begin setting up your freelance schedule by establishing regular work hours. Although no one is going to care if you start a few minutes early or late, work toward getting into your office at a specific time. Also plan to remain working for a specific number of hours each day. Schedule your work breaks and your daily lunch period.

Because most freelancers tend to be creative people, time management often works differently for them. In particular, organizing skills may be different or unusual. Creative people often keep stacks of stuff on their desks, rather than having the material filed away. This doesn't make a creative person wrong, just different. Whatever works for you is fine, just be sure it works for you.

If you are spending too much time searching for one particular item or a piece of paper, then you need to change your organizational techniques. If you cannot get your work done because of the way you are scheduling your

> **Bright Idea**
>
> Establishing a routine is one of the best ways to be productive. One of the reasons you might choose to be a freelancer—getting away from a daily routine schedule—may ironically be one of the things that helps you get your work done on time. Develop a work schedule that works for you.

work, then you need to change your schedule. Recognize what is working and what is not. Whatever is not working, you need to change.

It is up to you to manage your time properly. The more you can increase your productivity in your established work period, the more successful you will be as a freelancer. Some ways you can manage your time better include:

1. *Eliminate clutter.* Some people tend to thrive in clutter, but the more you can eliminate it or manage it, the more time you will have available.

2. *Maintain one calendar.* Don't keep multiple calendars. Have one master calendar that includes both your personal and business appointments.

3. *Throw away stuff you don't need or read.* If you have magazines you have not looked at for the past 30 days, file or store them away. Toss those that you never will look at again. If you do need something from a past issue of a magazine or newspaper, you will likely find it faster online or in a library than in massive piles in your office.

4. *Open your mail beside your wastebasket.* Throw away everything you can.

5. *Use highlighters.* They can identify important facts or information on a document.

6. *Use Post-It® Notes* to identify important documents.

7. *File away those things you will need to locate and use again.*

8. *Set a time each week to straighten and organize your work area.* This is your chance to get things back in order. Taking the time to get things back into shape often will improve your productivity.

9. *Mark your calendar with blocks of time to do specific routine tasks.* For example, set aside two times each month to pay your bills and maintain your accounting. It may only take one hour each time, but set a time on your schedule for these activities. Don't pay bills or issue statements until it is your chosen time slot. Then stop and complete that work. Building specific time blocks into your work schedule can vastly improve your productivity.

Freelance Business Basics

Whether you are moonlighting as a freelancer to supplement your current income or are working as a full-time freelancer, the one thing you must do is operate as a legitimate business. By taking the time and effort to set up a correctly formed business, you can eliminate later problems.

Legal Structure

Most freelancers start as a sole proprietorship. They do so because it

- is a fast way to begin freelancing operations.
- requires no special approval.

- is easy to change to another business form later.

Partnerships are not common for freelancers, especially those just starting. They sometimes occur later, after a freelancer has completed many assignments and has learned of another freelancer nearby with a similar or complimentary style. Formal partnerships, especially those that legally bind each partner, typically come later in a freelancing career. On the other hand, informal partnerships, such as those in which freelancers subcontract work, are quite common and can occur anytime the primary freelancer acquires too much work or needs help to get a portion of a project completed. Subcontracting is not a legal partnership, as far as ownership of a freelancing business is concerned. It is merely a method to get work completed for a client.

Before entering into any binding partnership, it is important to put together a legal, written partnership agreement. The agreement should include such things as how the partnership will be dissolved, what happens to existing clients, and who is responsible for specific tasks. You must also fully understand your liabilities and responsibilities as a partner. Your partner could do something, and in the eyes of the law, you could be held responsible for your partner's actions. For example, your partner may agree with you to pay taxes, but if your partner fails to do so, you may be held liable and responsible for any unpaid amount. Listen closely to your attorney's advice about your responsibilities as a partner in a business.

Corporations are sometimes created by an active freelancer. All the money received from the freelancer's clients is paid to the corporation, and the corporation then dispenses funds. In essence, you, the freelancer, become an employee of your own corporation. Taxes are paid before you receive your money in the form of a paycheck.

There are some advantages of owning a corporation and being an employee of your corporation. You may end up paying less in taxes. The corporation can purchase items you need for your business. Some of the disadvantages of operating as a corporation are that you have more forms and paperwork to be filed with the IRS and your state and local tax authorities. Never form a corporation without first consulting your attorney and your tax advisor. Fully understand your rights, duties, and obligations.

Some potential clients are more likely to use your services if you are a corporation, rather than a sole proprietor. The reason is that they contract with a corporation and not you as individual. By doing so, they can avoid any claims of workers'

Smart Tip

Tip...

It is often best to form or commence a corporation at the beginning of a tax year, such as January 1. Switching from a sole proprietor to a corporation is likely to be less complicated if you end a sole proprietorship on December 31 and start operating a corporation on January 1.

compensation or pension rights, or any claim demanding benefits an employee might expect. As your freelancing business grows, consider this as a reason to form a corporation.

Most freelancers start their freelancing business as a sole proprietorship. It is fast and easy, and takes little time. Forming a corporation costs money, requires approval from the state, and necessitates advice from experts.

Tax Identification Number

To get paid by a client, you must provide them with a tax identification number. For most individuals, this is a social security number. But with identify fraud rampant, it does not make sense to publish your social security number randomly via your invoices. You can solve this problem by applying for a tax identification number from the Internal Revenue Service. For sole proprietors as well as other legal entities, this is an Employer Identification Number (EIN). You may apply and use an EIN even if you have no employees. See the IRS publication 1635, *Understanding Your Employer Identification Number (EIN)* for more information.

You can obtain an EIN via the internet; use the IRS web site at www.irs.gov. Once all the necessary fields are completed on the online form, preliminary validation is performed. A provisional EIN is issued after the successful online submission. While this EIN can be used to open a bank account, apply for a business license, make a tax payment, or file a paper tax return, it will not be available for use on any IRS electronic system, such as e-File or TIN matching, for approximately seven to ten days.

You can get an EIN immediately by calling the IRS at (800) 829–4933 Monday through Friday, from 7 A.M. to 10 P.M. (local time).

You can also receive an EIN by completing Form SS-4, *Application for Employer Identification Number*, and faxing it to the IRS for processing. The IRS fax numbers are provided in the Form SS-4 instructions. Finally, you can obtain an EIN by completing the Form SS-4 and mailing it to the IRS service center address listed on the form instructions. By mailing the completed Form SS-4 to the appropriate service center, you can obtain an EIN within four to six weeks.

Business License

Depending on your location, you may be required to obtain a business license. Some locales require them; others do not. A quick telephone call to your local municipality, city hall, or county courthouse will tell you if you need a license. Many times, freelancing businesses are not required to be licensed. However, that is not universal, and you could be breaking the law by offering freelancing services without registering or obtaining a license. Find out what your local regulations are, and then follow the law.

3

Get Set Up
The Home Office

Writing businesses are often started at home. Indeed, most freelance writers work in a home office. Only highly specialized writers that must meet with a steady stream of clients establish offices not in their homes. For example, freelancers who prepare resumes and cover letters for those seeking employment often opt to establish a small office so their clients do not come to their homes. Still, most freelancers prefer to work from their home offices whenever possible.

Advantages of Working from a Home Office

There are several distinct advantages to setting up and operating from a home office. Some may be important to you; indeed, they may actually be the reasons why you are attracted to operating a freelance business.

Lower Overhead

A home office offers you low monthly overhead. When you rent an office outside of your home, you have additional monthly expenses. You do not need to write out rent checks or pay for extra energy costs when you operate from a home office. That's money that you don't spend; money that passes right to your bottom line. In other words, you make more money by not having the overhead of paying rent each month.

Tax Friendly

Your home office offers some tax-friendly benefits. Expenses you have now may become tax deductible once you establish your freelance business and conduct operations from your home office. The monthly electric, heat, cooling, water, sewerage, and trash service bills may become partially deductible. Even a cleaning service, usually considered a personal expense, may become partially deductible. You are entitled to deduct expenses even if you rent your home. If you are buying the property, you might be able to depreciate a portion of property value.

Your tax advisor can determine the amount that might be deductible as legitimate home office expenses. You would have to pay these expenses anyway. By carefully following the IRS rules for establishing a home office, you can often deduct expenses that were not deductible prior to establishing your business.

The trick is to comply fully with the Internal Revenue Service (IRS) regulations and document the business use of your property. Consult your tax advisor. You can also learn more about home office deductions directly

Tip...

Smart Tip
Because freelancers typically work from their homes, it is not difficult to establish your legitimate use of a home office and to qualify for the home office deduction.

from the IRS by reading Publication 587, *Business Use of Your Home*. It is available from any IRS office or from www.irs.gov.

Home Comfort

Working from home offers all the comforts and nuances of your daily home life. You waste no time traveling to work. There is no commute. There is no requirement for any special, expensive office wardrobe. Coffee breaks are as easy as a walk to your kitchen. You can wash your laundry while working. Lunch expenses are nonexistent; you can raid your refrigerator rather than spend money each day at a restaurant.

Easier to Establish

It takes less time to set up a home office than it does to establish an out-of-the-home office. There is no searching for the right location, need to consult an attorney on the lease, or reason to contact custodial services, security alarm companies, or office coffee services.

Less Expensive to Furnish

When you are renting office space, it is likely that you will need modern and often expensive furniture, just to keep up with other tenants. The property owner or manager might expect or require a specific style of furniture. Writers usually enjoy a bit of leeway because of the popular conception of being creative and freestyle. But that doesn't mean the property owner will allow an office to look like a stand at a local flea market.

Your home office, however, can be furnished cheaply and inexpensively. Anything goes as far as furniture is concerned. You can use an old desk and a dilapidated easy chair as part of your furnishings. Seldom, if ever, will clients see your work area. Your office only needs to be functional and comfortable to your standards. You do not need to furnish it to impress potential or current clients. Don't fall into the trap of over-spending for furniture for your home office. Functional, basic furniture is all you need.

Disadvantages of Working from a Home Office

For most freelancers, a home office is the preferred place to work. Although there are many advantages, there are also reasons why you might want to consider not setting up your work space in your home.

Distractions

One of the biggest problems of working at home is the ease of being distracted. Television, chores, and interruptions can cause breaks in your productivity. You need to develop and maintain discipline to get your work completed on schedule. Household chores—from cleaning to laundry—are always close by, and it is easy to divert your attention to non-work tasks. Some freelancers find it difficult to be working on projects when errands, shopping, or vacuuming needs to be done.

Work Is Ever-Present

With a home office, your work is always there, right where you live. Pending jobs and projects are never far away. Unlike an outside office, having your work so close may force you to work longer hours just because it is convenient to do so. If you did not have the work so close, you would very likely not do it during your downtime because you would not drive to the office to work.

Meeting Clients

It may, at times, be inconvenient not to be able to have clients meet in your office. This is particularly true if you must stop work and travel to your client's office (or some other neutral location). It can be frustrating when the meetings are short, and it takes more time to prepare for and travel to the meeting.

Setting Up Your Office

Creating a home office is fast and easy. You may already have done so, or at least partially started the process. If you have not yet started, you can set up your office quickly. It should not take more than a day to get most of the work done.

Your home office should be set up in its own room (rather than a corner or part of any other room). One of the simplest elements you need is a door. Your work area must be a place where you can go and close off the rest of the world. As an active freelancer, you will constantly be working on new and different projects. Your primary goal is to get the work done. Often that work is performed under the stress of fast-approaching deadlines. You cannot have interruptions from family members or friends. Having a work area with a door allows you to set up barriers to those who would interrupt your work.

The most important part of your home office is your desk or worktable. It is from here that all other functions of your office radiate. Position your desk at a central and comfortable place. Make sure it offers easy accessibility to the electrical outlets and telephone lines. You should also consider its proximity to windows and available lighting. As a freelancer, you will spend many long and important hours at your desk. What you do there generates your paychecks.

You could spend thousands of dollars on new equipment and furnishings, but none of these expenditures will insure your success as a freelancer, nor would they make sense. You would do better to save your money for rainy days, marketing, and financial emergencies.

Computer

After you've determined where to position your desk or worktable, the next most important piece of equipment is a computer, which you probably own. (If you do not own one or own an outdated system, you need to go shopping.) It is probably next to impossible to operate your freelancing business without a personal computer. From creating the work your clients want and need to keeping track of business expenses, your computer will be your primary piece of business equipment. And, of course, few clients today would consider hiring a freelancer who does not have the ability to produce and deliver electronic media files or communicate via e-mail.

Desktop versus Notebook

One of your earliest computing decisions is to decide if you should use a desktop or a notebook computer. There are advantages and disadvantages to each.

Desktop units cost less than notebooks. They often offer higher capacity for less money. You can purchase more memory, more disk storage, and a faster processor. You can add a larger monitor, and easily expand your system by adding additional memory or disk drives.

Notebook computers offer portability. Today's notebooks have longer lasting batteries, making it easier to work in many different locations. Most notebooks have wireless capability, so it's easy to connect to a computer network (or the internet). You can work at your client's location, at a coffee shop or restaurant, or in a library. It is often advantageous to take along your computer work files to meetings, which is easy with a notebook computer. On the downside, a notebook computer also is more vulnerable to theft or damage. Important files or information could be lost forever if you have not backed them up.

The best solution for the freelancer is to have two computers: a notebook and desktop. This combination assures flexibility and a backup. As a professional, you cannot tell your clients that you cannot deliver work because your computer is down or not working. You should have a backup system, and for maximum capability, it makes sense to have both types of computers. If you cannot afford both, start with a laptop, if you can afford it. If you are starting on a shoestring budget, then go for an inexpensive desktop model.

Windows PC versus Mac

When purchasing a computer, another decision is a personal computer (PC) or a Mac. PCs use Microsoft's Windows Operating System. Macs are manufactured by Apple, and use the Macintosh Operating System. PCs usually cost less than Macs and generally have more software available. Macs offer sophisticated graphics and ease of use.

Fanatic computer owners could forever debate the issue of which to use. Forgetting the passionate debate on both sides, your decision should be straightforward and based on business. Go with the platform that 90 percent of your clients use. If most of your clients use PCs, then you should use a PC. Or if your area of expertise means that most of your clients use Mac, then you should use a Mac.

Transferring data between PCs and Macs is not as difficult as it once was. Most Mac users that use your services can process and use files you create on a PC. PC users often have more difficulty with Macintosh-created files.

If you are not sure which to select, you are probably safer choosing the PC.

Other Computer Hardware

You need more than just a computer to work. You also need some extra hardware, commonly called *peripherals*. Some of the peripherals you might need are:

1. *Monitor.* If you are using a desktop computer, a monitor is necessary. If you are using a notebook computer, a larger screen is a nice extra. Purchase as large a monitor with the best resolution that your budget permits. When purchasing a laptop computer, buy the model with the larger screen.

2. *Printer.* You need at least one printer for your computer. Printers are drastically less expensive than they were just a decade ago. As you work to establish your freelance writing business, you probably need to purchase an updated printer with a heavier capacity. Before buying any printer, always check the price of the replacement toner or ink cartridges. Your purchase should be partially based on those costs.

   - *Laser printer (black toner).* Laser printers are available for less than $200. As a professional freelancer, a laser printer is not a luxury but a necessity. A small, personal laser printer can produce reams of printed pages inexpensively. For some freelance writers, this is as much printer as they need. Color should be avoided in most manuscripts.

   - *Color printer.* There are both color inkjet printers and color laser printers. The inkjet printers have drastically reduced prices. Smaller, inexpensive units are often offered for $40 or less by major retailers. Color laser printers are available from $350. Adding a color printer to your office is certainly affordable. Color presentations impress your clients. Color cartridges, however, are more expensive than black toner, and can be very expensive per copy. Consider the costs of refills before making a purchase.

- *Label printer*. Label printers also save time. They range in price from $100 to $200. Many of the models allow you to create U.S. postage stamps directly from your computer.

3. *Scanner*. A scanner allows you to copy documents, illustrations, photographs, and images into your computer. Many models also offer Optical Character Recognition (OCR). This allows you to copy printed pages or documents into a readable file. You can then import that file into your word processor. Scanners generally range in price from $50 to $300. Many include a handy feature that turns your computer into a simple copying machine.

4. *Fax*. Most computers have the capability to send and receive faxes through a modem. Some industries still rely heavily on faxes, while others seldom use them. The cost of a modem that can send and receives faxes is minimal. Most current computers have this capability.

> **Tip...**
>
> **Smart Tip**
> You no longer need a dedicated telephone line or a fax machine to send and receive faxes. You can send faxes via e-mail. Services such as efax (www.efax.com) allow you to receive faxes anytime you access your e-mail. If you must fill out forms and fax them, you need either a standard fax machine or a scanner attached to your computer. Services like those from efax.com cost less to maintain than a fax machine and a separate telephone line.

Telephone Service

All businesses need telephone service. Your freelance business is no exception. Freelancers use the telephone to contact clients, prospects or potential clients, and sources. Depending on your work assignments, you may be on the telephone for extended periods of time. Some of the features you need to consider when thinking about your telephone service include:

- *Long distance*. You will more than likely need long distance telephone service. It is not uncommon to conduct interviews and business across the country. You need affordable long distance calling. Some companies now have unlimited long distance service for a flat rate. Another alternative is long-distance calling cards, which offer service for only a few cents each minute. The rates have dropped over the past years, while quality has improved.

- *Voice-mail service.* You will need voice-mail service so your telephone is answered when you are not in your office or busy working on assignments. Your voice-mail box should be accessible from anywhere.
- *Conference calling.* Depending on your assignments, you may need the capability to make conference calls. Telephone meetings are common. As a freelancer, you may need to speak with your client and others at the same time.
- *Wired telephone.* Your primary telephone should not be a wireless model, but rather a wired telephone. You do not want to be talking to a client or a source and have your conversation fade out or be interrupted by radio static.
- *Cell phone.* Most freelancers have a cell phone. Replacing pagers as a way for quick contact, the cell phone is an important communications tool for the busy freelancer. Some freelancers use a cell phone as their business telephone. Others use a standard telephone service but forward their calls to their cell phones when they are out of the home office. Consider the service plans and the terms of commitment. Some cell phone service providers require a two-year service plan. If you already have a cell phone, you should probably be able to use it in your freelance business.

Digital Recorder

Still called a "tape recorder" by some people, a digital recorder has no recording tape. Instead, voices are recorded on a computer chip and replayed when needed. You can download a computer file from your digital recorder onto your computer, keeping your interviews and meeting notes in electronic format. They can be retrieved at any time.

You can send your digitally recorded file away via e-mail and have it transcribed. A quick search of "digital transcription service" on any internet search engine locates hundreds of companies that provide this service. Most can turn around a digital file within 24 to 48 hours, with incredible accuracy. The transcription is delivered in a usable word processing file. Digital recorders range from $50 to $200. Depending on the type of freelancing you do, you may find a digital recorder is an important part of your necessary small tools. Today's digital recorders are quite compact, generally smaller than a pack of cards.

Internet Connectivity

Just as you need a business telephone number, you also need access to the internet. Internet access is not a luxury item for a freelancer. It is a necessity. You can get easily get internet access via

- dial-up (you dial across a telephone line using your computer modem),
- DSL service (provided by your telephone company),
- cable connection (provided by your cable TV company), or
- radio or wireless (available in some parts of the country, requires you to have special send/receive capability on your computer).

Internet Activity

You will spend a lot of your time on the internet. You will use it to seek clients, conduct research, and communicate via e-mail to prospects and clients. For freelancers, connecting to the internet and working is as common as other businesspeople walking into their offices and flipping on the lights to begin work.

E-Mail

It is nearly impossible to function as a freelancer unless you have an active e-mail account. In today's freelancing world, e-mail is usually the primary method of communicating with clients. Just as you need a telephone to operate a business, so do you need an e-mail address. You have several options when considering an e-mail address. These include using

- web-based e-mail,
- Internet Service Provider (ISP) e-mail, and
- private domain.

Web-based e-mail is often free. Many of the major web companies offer e-mail service, and plenty of free storage. Some of the sources of free web-based e-mail are Yahoo.com, Hotmail.com, and Gmail.com. The advantage of using web-based e-mail, in addition to being free, is that your e-mail address can remain constant.

Always consider what type of image your e-mail address presents. You should have a reasonable e-mail address, such as

- gs@aol.com,
- gsheldon@earthlink.com,
- gshel1156@msn.com, or
- george@sheldononline.com.

Your address should not be offensive in any way. Questionable e-mail addresses that have a sexual connotation, suggest questionable activities, or are just plain distasteful do not present a professional image. In other words, they are likely to hurt your freelance business. Some bad examples of addresses are:

- womanmaster@aol.com,
- bigfanny@earthlink.com,
- thehacker@msn.com, and
- a-real-ass@compuserve.com.

Being cool is not the attribute you want your e-mail address to convey. You are a professional businessperson. Be careful with your online persona, especially as it relates to your freelance business image.

Smart Tip

Tip...

Send yourself an e-mail message to check the appearance. Reply to that e-mail to make sure everything in your setup is working properly.

Make sure your e-mail software is properly installed and set up. Make certain your name appears correctly in the From: box. Avoid From: text that says, "Another Frustrated Freelancer." Make sure you have your correct e-mail address in the return section so when a prospect or client attempts to reply, she can send a message to you without any effort.

Domain Registration

You may want to consider purchasing your own internet domain. With companies like www.godaddy.com or www.networksolutions.com, registering your domain is fast and inexpensive. Your domain is your own internet address. For example, if your name is John Smith and you live in Boulder, Colorado, you might register a domain name such as

Johnsmith.com,

Smithwrites.com,

Coloradowriting.com, or

Boulderwriter.com.

Once you purchase your domain name and register it, you can use your domain name on all your correspondence and business communications. You can establish your own e-mail accounts and maintain your online presence easily.

Web Site

By purchasing your own domain name, you can then establish your own web site. Your web site can become a primary tool in your marketing and your search for clients. (This is covered later.) Because of the low cost of purchasing a domain name (less than $20) and hosting a web site (less than $5 a month), most freelancers should consider this option.

Computer Software

Computers do not work without software. It's like buying a DVD player and never inserting a DVD. Your DVD player is useless without DVDs, and your computer is useless without software. To get the most out of your computer and all the extras (hardware), you need software.

Microsoft Office

In today's business world, Microsoft Office® is the predominate software in use. There are other competitive products available, but Office, which bundles various Microsoft programs, is king. Because of packaging, marketing, pricing, and functionality, Office is widely used on business computers. Office most commonly includes a word processor (Word), a spreadsheet (Excel), a presentation program (PowerPoint), and an e-mail/contact manager/calendar (Outlook). Over the years, however, Microsoft has changed Office and publishes versions that include Access (a database program) or Publisher (a desktop publishing program). The version you purchase determines which Microsoft programs are included.

One of the reasons Office has become so dominate is that it is cheaper to buy software in a package than as individual pieces. Products like Word can be purchased individually from Microsoft, but the price drops drastically when it is purchased in a bundle.

Word

Microsoft's Word is the world's leading word processor. It is now the standard, and any file you produce for a client must be Word compatible. If you are using a word processor other than Word, you need to be able to convert your files to Word format.

Excel

Microsoft Excel is the world's leading spreadsheet. Just as Word dominates word processing, Excel dominates spreadsheet programming. A spreadsheet can be used for all kinds of things, from financial calculations to database use. All spreadsheet files must be delivered to clients compatible with Excel.

Accounting Software

You need to acquire bookkeeping or accounting software. QuickBooks from Intuit Software (www.quickbooks.com) dominates the small business market. Other competitive products, such as Peachtree, are available. If you are going to consult with a tax advisor, be sure to check first with your advisor to make sure your software is compatible with what he or she uses.

Antivirus

Because of the proliferation of viruses, worms, spyware, Trojans, malware, and other malicious attempts by demented programmers and hackers to destroy another's computer or steal information, anti-virus software is a necessity. It is a necessity both for you and the person receiving your e-mail. The last thing you need to do is send a virus to a client or customer via e-mail. You need anti-virus software that is properly installed and working on your computer. This means that the software is constantly updating itself, receiving and installing the most recent updates onto your computer. Outdated antivirus software is useless. You need to make certain that your software is working properly.

Computer viruses, by definition, are stealthy and hidden, constantly spreading themselves. Attaching themselves to an e-mail message or using a stored e-mail address to spread and infect another computer is the nature of the virus. Should you send a virus, your e-mail address will probably be blocked by the recipient's e-mail software. Sending a computer virus is not a good way to establish a new business relationship.

Bright Idea

Check with your internet provider before you buy an anti-virus program. Many offer free anti-virus software as part of their internet service. You don't have to purchase software; it's free as part of your monthly subscription. And it is constantly updated and upgraded. Should you have any trouble installing it, your Internet Service Provider (ISP) will provide technical support and service.

Beware!

Free web-based e-mail, such as that provided by Google, Yahoo, Microsoft, and others, may not cost you anything, but it is often laced with advertisements or other messages that your clients and prospects will see. When you use free e-mail accounts, remember that you cannot control what is added to the end of your messages. Free is not always best, especially when you are operating a business.

E-Mail Software

You need some kind of software to handle your e-mail, unless you are using web site e-mail. Different kinds of e-mail software are available at all prices. Test your setup by sending an e-mail to yourself to make sure the format looks good and is acceptable.

Other Useful Software

You will more than likely need other software, based on the type of freelancing you are

Smart Tip

Many software publishers grant a 30-day free trial of their software, so you can test their product before buying.

doing. You may need software products from Adobe (www.adobe.com). Adobe publishes Adobe Acrobat®, the dominant program for reading PDF documents and, more importantly, versions that allow PDF documents to be corrected. Adobe also publishes PhotoShop (used by professional photographers to enhance digital photos) and DreamWeaver (a web site building program). You might also use other software programs, tools, or utilities to produce the products needed by your clients. Each freelancer has her own needs, based on the kind of work she is doing. Fortunately, it is also common for those who hire freelancers to provide expensive software programs or to make arrangements for their purchase through timely payments.

Never use pirated, stolen, or unlicensed software. To do so sends the message to your clients and prospects that you are a thief and someone that cannot be trusted.

Furniture

Your home office needs furniture to make it functional and to help you get your work completed. Each office can be furnished to the liking of the freelancer, but functionality is primary. If you can't get your work done, the furniture is the wrong choice. Furnish your office so it is an inviting place to work.

You can buy new or used furniture. You can use what you already have. Because you will seldom, if ever, have clients visit your home office, it is not important to furnish it as if you were attempting to influence clients and prospects with expensive, contemporary furnishings.

Desk

All offices need a desk of some kind where you position your telephone, computer, stationery, and office supplies. Your work is completed at the desk. There are, of course, many options available. A desk really can be a flat surface with legs. Some freelancers begin working off an old table. Don't overinvest here, especially when getting started. As your freelancing business turns profitable, you can then purchase a more extravagant desk, if you want.

Chair

The most important part of your home office is not the furniture, but rather you. Without you, there is no freelancing business. So one of the most important things you can purchase for yourself is a good chair. Don't be cheap or impatient over the purchase of an office chair. Shop around and try various models out. Get one that fits you, your preferences, and your work style. Some people prefer armless chairs, other prefer chairs with arms. Some like high backs, and others like chairs with lower backs. You will be spending innumerable hours at your desk in the chair. Purchase one that helps you endure those long hours of work.

Lighting

Make certain your home office has sufficient lighting for you to work. Desk lamps are inexpensive, and investment there can make a big difference in the quality of your work. Good lighting helps you edit and locate necessary fixes and changes in your work.

Filing Cabinets

Keep your work area organized by filing papers, documents, catalogs, and other information that you gather. A filing cabinet is an inexpensive way to organize and have the documents you need at your fingertips when you need them. Taking the extra time to file documents saves hours of lost time on a frantic search to find that one piece of paper.

Two-drawer file cabinets are often available for about $50. They can be positioned strategically in your office, and you can place supplies, printer, or other important tools on their tops.

Bookshelves

Standard bookshelves help to organize and maintain order in your office. They can store not only your books but also magazines, supplies, and other items that can be neatly arranged on their shelves.

Office Supplies

The active freelancer needs a small stash of basic office supplies: envelopes, pens, pencils, paper, file folders, pads, paper clips, and similar items. You also need a dictionary and other reference books. When working, the last thing you want to do is stop your production and travel to the local office supply store for a small office item, or go online to search a word or grammar style easily found in a reference manual.

You can save time and shopping by using online ordering from major office supply retailers. All offer free next-day delivery service. Some of the major retailers are:

- Quill Corporation, www.quill.com

- Corporate Express, www.corporateexpress.com
- Staples, www.staples.com
- OfficeMax, www.officemax.com
- OfficeDepot, www.officedepot.com

Miscellaneous Niceties

Several other items make your work at your desk easier: wireless keyboard, optical mouse (wireless), and mouse pad. These little extras make it easier to adjust and work in your office. You will be spending many hours there, so those little things you can do to make yourself more comfortable while you work will make you more productive.

4

Legal
Issues

As a freelancer, you often create what is collectively known as intellectual property, or sometimes IP. Buried deep in the U.S. Constitution, the nation's forefathers thought it was important to encourage and protect those who create intellectual property.

Understanding Copyright

In Article I, Section 8, the U.S. Constitution specifically gives Congress the power . . . "To promote the progress of science and useful arts, by securing for limited times to authors and inventors the exclusive right to their respective writings and discoveries . . ." It is within those few words that Congress gains the exclusive power to establish copyright law.

The subject of intellectual property and copyright is complicated and extensive. Some attorneys specialize in this area. Clearly, copyright law easily fills volumes and is far beyond the scope of this book. But simply stated, realize that what you create as a freelancer is often covered under copyright law. You can either retain your copyright or you can sell those rights.

Clients often require or request the purchase of all the rights you have, transferring those rights to them. After they pay you, you have no further right to the property. Clients may also ask for specific rights—and allow you to retain all others. For example, a magazine may ask for First North American Serial Rights. That means it is purchasing the right to be the first one to publish your article. After it purchases those rights, you are free to sell the work again to anyone you want. The only thing you cannot do is sell First North American Serial Rights, because they were already sold. Many writers sell either reprint (the right to reprint the article) or one-time rights (the right to use the material one time).

Some basic rules when dealing with copyright are:

1. Under the United States Copyright Act (found at Title 17 of the U.S. Code), creators of original materials are granted exclusive rights, generally referred to as the creator's "copyrights."

2. There are both civil and criminal penalties for those that infringe a copyright.

3. Copyright protection exists from the time the work is created, and immediately becomes the property of the author who created the work. Only the author, or those deriving their rights through the author, can rightfully claim copyright.

4. Copyright protection is provided to the authors of "original works of authorship, including literary, dramatic, musical, artistic, and certain other intellectual works."

5. Copyright protection is extended to *both* published and unpublished works.

6. Copyright laws provide for "work made for hire." In these cases, work made for hire allow the employer, and not the writer, to be considered the author and the owner of the copyright.

Contracts and Agreements

Freelancers must understand and use the copyright laws correctly. Some material that a freelancer creates is worthless, other than to the freelancer's client. For example, creating a two-page resume is unlikely to be worth anything beyond the fee paid for the work. As a freelancer in this situation, you would probably not affect your income by assigning all rights to the client.

However, in other instances, protecting your rights is wise. Suppose you created a magazine article and submitted it for publication. You could sell all rights, which means you own nothing after receiving payment. Or you could sell just those rights necessary to allow the publication of the article, holding onto all other rights. This usually makes sense. The general rule is to give up just those rights necessary to get the work, and nothing more.

It might be far less complicated to assign all rights to your client. But what if W. Bruce Cameron had done so? He wrote an article called *8 Simple Rules for Dating My Teenage Daughter*. If he had sold all rights, he would not have been able to sell a book with the same title, which led to a television show that starred John Ritter and Katey Segal.

The American Society of Journalists and Authors (ASJA) recommends that freelancers not agree to accepting all-rights or work made for hire agreements for magazine and newspaper work, except in very special cases. ASJA says, "Remember, as an independent professional writer, you do not 'sell' an article. You license specific uses of it."

ASJA also reminds freelancers, "A license to cover electronic rights, like licenses for any extra rights, should be based on this principle: All uses beyond first print publication must be separately licensed and separately compensated."

Work Made for Hire

Any work made for hire (WMFH) agreement must be in writing to be deemed valid. Verbal WMFH agreements are invalid. They are not enforceable in court. Most often, the freelancer's client will have a document ready, seeking all rights under a work made for hire agreement. Other times, you, as the freelancer, need to provide the agreement to the client.

The common language of a standard WMFH agreement is given in the Standard Work Made for Hire Agreement on page 34.

Standard Work Made for Hire Agreement

THE AUTHOR AND THE CLIENT AGREE THAT:

Title and Copyright Assignment

(a) Author and Client intend this to be a contract for services and each considers the products and results of the services to be rendered by Author hereunder (the "Work") to be a work made for hire. Author acknowledges and agrees that the Work (and all rights therein, including, without limitation, copyright) belongs to and shall be the sole and exclusive property of the Client.

(b) If for any reason the Work would not be considered a work made for hire under applicable law, Author does hereby sell, assign, and transfer to the Client, its successors and assigns, the entire right, title and interest in and to the copyright in the Work and any registrations and copyright applications relating thereto and any renewals and extensions thereof, and in and to all works based upon, derived from, or incorporating the Work, and in and to all income, royalties, damages, claims and payments now or hereafter due or payable with respect thereto, and in and to all causes of action, either in law or in equity for past, present, or future infringement based on the copyrights, and in and to all rights corresponding to the foregoing throughout the world.

(c) If the Work is one to which the provisions of 17 U.S.C. 106A apply, the Author hereby waives and appoints the Client to assert on the Author's behalf the Author's moral rights or any equivalent rights regarding the form or extent of any alteration to the Work (including, without limitation, removal or destruction) or the making of any derivative works based on the Work, including, without limitation, photographs, drawings or other visual reproductions or the Work, in any medium, for the client's purposes.

(d) Author agrees to execute all papers and to perform such other proper acts as the Client may deem necessary to secure for Client or its designee the rights herein assigned.

Licensing Specific Rights

Just as a written agreement is used for work made for hire assignments, a written agreement should be used when the freelancer is licensing copyrighted material to a client. By doing so, it eliminates any future misunderstanding. Normally, licensing agreements are handled in a simple letter. The wording, within a paragraph, might be something like:

> For the fee of $1,250, we have agreed to grant you First North American Serial Rights to my article entitled, First Friday. We have further agreed that these rights are in effect for one year. If you do not publish First Friday within that time, the right to publish reverts to me. We also agree that the fee is nonrefundable, should you not publish my article. You have not purchased any other rights to my material.

Always put your licensing agreements in writing. There should never be any exceptions to this simple rule.

Registering Your Copyrighted Material

You might ask, "Isn't copyright registration an expensive pain?" Actually, it's neither as costly nor as onerous as you may think. Registration costs $45, but you can gang articles on a single application to save on fees and drudgery. If you're a prolific article writer, the cost per story is quite low. To meet the within-three-months requirement, you need to file four times a year, each time listing your previous three months' published work. Four filings and $180 give you maximum protection on a year's output of freelancing.

To group register, you need two official U.S. Copyright Office forms:

1. Form TX for nondramatic literary works (the streamlined Short Form TX may usually be used for a single work);
2. Form GR/CP for grouping published works on a single application.

You can obtain the forms directly from the Copyright Office by phoning (202) 707-9100 (available 24 hours a day). Leave a message and in about two to three weeks, your forms will arrive via the U.S. mail. You can also download them from the Copyright Office's web site. Use a good grade of 8.5-by-11-inch white paper, use both sides of the sheet, and match the layout of the originals.

On Form GR/CP, list articles chronologically, from earliest to latest, numbering the lines consecutively; no more than 12 months may separate the first from the last.

The Copyright Office's separate instruction sheets say that you must include the entire magazine or newspaper section in which each submitted article appeared—but that needn't actually be done. The Office advises that you may instead submit simple tear sheets or even photocopies. Just be sure to include with your application a letter asking that the Copyright Office "please accept the enclosed tear sheets [or photo-copies] as part of ongoing special relief from the deposit requirement." This kind of request is routinely granted by the Copyright Office. Enclose a check for $45, payable to Register of Copyrights. Mail your application to Register of Copyrights, Library of Congress, Washington, DC 20559-6000. Certified mail, return receipt requested, isn't a bad idea, but you can also use the Postal Service's Delivery Confirmation.

It usually takes about 12 to 16 weeks for your copyright registration to be recorded. You may also submit the manuscript versions, but you may not use form GR/CP, nor may you mix published and unpublished works together. The copyright office allows you to group unpublished works using form TX. Use a descriptive title for the group, such as "unpublished writings, Jan–Mar 2009."

For more information about U.S. copyright contact:

U.S. Copyright Office

101 Independence Avenue SE

Washington, DC 20559-6000

Phone: (202) 707-3000

8:30 A.M. to 5 P.M. Eastern time, Monday through Friday

http://lcweb.loc.gov/copyright

www.copyright.gov

Launching a Freelance Writing Business

You've decided that freelance writing is for you. The office is set up. You have your telephone numbers and your e-mail account. You are all ready to start. The only thing you need is a client. Without customers, you are not really in business. It's the one thing that you must find consistently if you want to stay in business. The moment you and a client connect, you have an assignment and you're a freelancer.

Finding Customers

With many businesses, you can advertise to find customers. You can purchase advertising space on billboards or in newspapers. You can become a radio show sponsor or purchase spots on television. You might consider advertising in the Yellow Pages. However, in freelance writing, none of these traditional methods of business advertising works.

You can try buying traditional advertising, but you will find that there is little, if any, return on your investment. For any number of reasons, the people (clients) who purchase freelancing services do not do so following exposure to traditional advertising. Perhaps advertising would work—if you spent enough money—but you would need to make exorbitant purchases to get any return.

So how does the new freelance writing business find customers if most traditional advertising is ineffective? The good news is that the best methods of finding new clients have little, low, or no costs. Marketing your services—making potential clients aware of your availability—is the best method to building your business.

When You Should Advertise

There are some exceptions to the no advertising rule. One freelance writing opportunity that works with advertising is resume and cover letter writing. Many freelancers offer resume writing services. Advertising that you are available to create effective resumes often returns more than enough to cover the cost of the advertising. The best place to advertise this service is the Sunday newspaper in the Help Wanted section, which often has a category for resume services.

A resume writing service often requires you to work quickly. A potential client calls because of an advertisement offering a job. The client needs to send a resume immediately for consideration. You can earn more by offering to write cover letters. In today's world, many resumes are submitted electronically, in Adobe Acrobat PDF format. This is yet another service that you can provide.

Providing Super Service Creates Referrals

Freelancing is a service business. You may later decide to create products and sell them to supplement your income. As a working freelancer, your primary business is to provide a service to a client. You work to complete the assignment. In essence, you are working to get yourself work. As soon as you do, you can take on more work. This is how most freelance writing businesses operate. It is a simple cycle.

One of the smartest things you can do is provide outstanding service to your clients. This service begins with the initial contact and runs through to the delivery of the final work. Always be at the service of your clients. Always ask how you can help them. Fast, on-time delivery will create more opportunities for you.

Good service is important for another reason. One of the key things you want from your clients is referrals. When you have a good working relationship with a current client, you can ask for referrals. It is common for a client to recommend a freelancer to a business associate. Sometimes the referral can be to another department or section within the same organization, while other times the referral may be to someone at another organization or company.

Referrals cost nothing. When a current customer refers you to someone else, there is an implied endorsement and a recommendation attached to the referral. It is easy to break the ice. With a simple phone call or e-mail message, you can quickly start the conversation with something like, "John Jackson recommended I contact you. I am a freelancer available for assignment. After I successfully completed a marketing campaign for John, he thought you might be interested in knowing about my services."

In freelancing, there is an old axiom. "You are only as good as your last job." Simply stated, it's easy to lose a client by doing a lousy job. Don't do bad work. Take on only what you can and still provide a top-quality service that clients want to recommend.

Getting the Word Out

In the early stages of a freelancing business, you should spend significant amounts of time looking for business. This means your initial work will not be completing freelance assignments, but rather spreading the world that you are in business and are seeking work.

The goal is to find work, but you want to do so with little expense and by telling everyone likely to hire you that you are available. A number of methods are useful to get you started.

Internet

The internet is probably the first place to look for assignments. It is a vast marketplace for any freelancer. Start by searching for those who are searching for you. The major search engines, such as Google, Yahoo!, MSN Search, and AltaVista, may reveal potential clients quickly. Searching for "writers wanted," "editor needed," or "proofreader sought" often provides lists of people to contact. Some of the listings will be older and outdated. Eliminate those that are likely to still be inactive and spend your time contacting the more recent listings.

Web Site

Establishing your own web site is a low-cost marketing technique. For $15, you can register your own domain name and purchase your first month's web hosting service. Domain discounters like godaddy.com offer registration for around $9 (for a year). They also offer web hosting, where you rent a small piece of a web server, for $4 a month. Many times, there are discounts available, making the initial start-up costs even cheaper.

Use your web site to offer information about you and your services. Be sure to register your site, after completion, with the search engines.

Before web sites and the internet, it would have cost you thousands of dollars to print a color brochure with multiple pages of information about yourself. Today, you can have an electronic version for $15, on a web site that costs less than $5 a month.

Blog

Another fast way to call attention to your freelancing business is to establish a blog. A blog is a user-generated web site where multiple entries are displayed in journal style, in a reverse chronological order. Blogs usually provide specialized commentary on a particular subject, such as food or politics.

Today, a typical blog combines text, images, and links to other blogs, web pages, and media related to its topic. The ability of readers to leave comments is also a standard feature of most blogs.

Establishing a blog is faster and easier than you may think. For example, www.blogger.com offers setup within minutes. As a Google web site, your entries are included in the Google

Smart Tip

Tip...

Building an effective blog might be more work than you first think. To get attention in the blogosphere, create links to other blogs (seek permission, which is an informal way of getting another blogger's attention). Don't set up a blog and forget it. It needs to be fed regularly. Many experts say blogs should be updated daily, and even several times each day. No one wants to read yesterday's newspaper.

search engine. Setting up and running a blog on Blogger.com costs nothing. It is a free service, and one that can get you noticed quickly on the internet.

Finding Work on Freelancing Sites

There are numerous web sites designed to help freelancers find work. Some of the sites offer advertisements or listings. You simply list yourself, describe your services, and wait until a buyer of freelancing contacts you. Some sites allow you to list yourself for free, while others charge a fee for the service.

Other sites allow those that need freelancing services to list their jobs. You, as a freelancer, look at the jobs and bid on the work. You can find some low paying work, but many of the jobs may not be wise to undertake. Because of low pay or extensive work, it may be best to move on to other work. But as a new freelancer, it makes sense to check these web sites and look for opportunities to build your resume.

Some web sites you should consider when looking for work are:

www.allfreelance.com

www.craigslist.com

www.dice.com

www.elance.com

www.freelancefree.com

www.freelancewriting.com

www.getgigs.com

www.gofreelance.com

www.guru.com

www.ifreelance.com

www.mediabistro.com

www.odesk.com

www.sologig.com

www.workbuggy.com

Smart Tip

Depending on your area of expertise and freelancing experience, you may find work from specific organizations. For example, freelance writers may find that joining a writers association gives access to a job board or provides a listing in a membership directory.

There are other sites, too. Web sites come and go, so it always pays to keep searching for new sites that might offer opportunities for you to pick up work and ongoing clients.

Conversation with Melanie Votaw

"I think a lot of people undersell themselves on Elance, but I suppose some of them don't have the credentials or the portfolio to get the higher paying work," freelancer

Melanie Votaw says. "I always do my best to make sure I never make less than $50 per hour, and that's my bare minimum. "I always strive for more than that and often get it."

Melanie is based in Brooklyn, New York. She is a busy book author, journalist, speaker, copywriter, and editor. She often uses Elance to find paying freelance work.

"There are certainly plenty of buyers on Elance who don't want to pay my rates," Melanie says. "But there are plenty who do. If you have a good portfolio, you can get those jobs."

Now a part of Elance for several years, Melaine explains that she has had the opportunity to do some sales copywriting (brochures, web sites, letters, press releases, etc.). "I hadn't done a great deal of that kind of writing, and I was interested in it." So she started her marketing process. "On my own site, I created "dummy" samples, which I think is an excellent way to start building your portfolio. If you haven't done it for someone else, make one up to show what you can do," Melanie says. "Elance helped me to build my copywriting portfolio."

"There are also people on Elance calling themselves writers who have no business doing so," Melanie muses. "I have been hired a couple of times to fix absolutely atrocious work by so-called professionals."

She says that you really have to weed through the listings to find the gems, but she has been hooked up with some fascinating people through Elance. "One of the more interesting was an attorney from Dallas who is a prominent speaker for firms and bar associations. He hired me to doctor a book that he has self-published and is selling at his speaking engagements. It was an absolute pleasure to work with him, and he was very pleased with the result," she reports, adding, "The pay was also quite good. I also wrote a speech for an exec that I really enjoyed producing. It was based on a rough outline, so it required a lot of creativity from me."

Melanie has found an ever-growing amount of work from the site. "I've written a few e-books and edited quite a few manuscripts (one on the Qu'ran). I've also taken on a few projects writing articles on subjects that I wanted to learn more about," she says.

"One of the things I like about this kind of work is that they're usually thrilled with the quality and don't ask for revisions," explains Melanie. "My hourly can end up being quite a bit higher than if I work for a magazine that nitpicks me to death. I have developed some expertise in new areas as a result of this work—yachts, for example. I never would have expected to be learning about yachts, but here I am!"

As is so typical of freelancers, Melanie has moved away from copywriting and is concentrating primarily on books. "I'm ghosting three at the moment," she says during an interview.

She has used other web sites to find work, including Mediabistro.com and Craigslist.com, but Elance is best. "Elance is a much higher quality site with many more listings, and I've gotten a substantial amount of work through it," says Melanie, who maintains her own web site at www.RuletheWord.com. "You do, of course, have to go through the listings and place bids. This takes a little bit of marketing time. And as I said, you have to weed through the 50 articles at $2 each listings."

Send Introductory Letters

Another fast and effective way for freelancers to find work is to send letters of introduction to potential clients. For example, if you are looking for public relations work, you might send letters of introduction to local nonprofits. See the Introductory Letter sample on page 44.

Samples

Create samples of the types of work that you can do. Copyright your samples, and distribute them by mail or via the internet. Put them on your web site (in PDF format created by using Adobe Acrobat). Samples are a great way to market your work and yourself. You are showing potential clients what you've done and what you are capable of producing.

Sample Introductory Letter

Potential Client
Name
Address

Get that work done now!
Freelancer Available for Big or Small Jobs

Dear _____ :

When you next consider your arrangements to get your annual community directory produced, I would welcome the opportunity to understand your requirements and situation.

I provide fast and effective freelance service. I can get your directory produced with minimal disruption to you. Cost-effective and with on-time delivery, I will also free your staff so it can do other important tasks. It makes great business sense for you to send this—and all your similar projects—out to my freelance service.

For a prompt quote or to discuss your needs, please call me at (717) 555-1212 or e-mail me mary@ready.com.

Yours sincerely,

Mary Ready

Rules You
Cannot Break

As a working freelancer, there are several rules that you simply cannot breach. If you do, you are opening yourself to litigation or perhaps criminal prosecution. Even worse, your integrity and honesty will be compromised.

It is often easy to find yourself in situations that provide opportunities for mistakes that could cause serious professional damage. No matter what type of writing service you offer, you must always take the high road, avoiding any question about your ethics.

The Client's Interest Comes First

Your first rule as a freelancer is that your client's interest must always come first. This seems like a simple rule and one everybody should follow. But the truth is, too many people do not put their client's interests above their own.

If you cannot do the work the client wants when he wants it, you should turn down the assignment. Sometimes you can't do the work because you don't have the time. Other times you might need special equipment or tools that you do not own, can't rent, or don't have easy access to. Sometimes, there are real or potential conflicts of interest.

Conflict of Interest

There are times when you must turn down work because there is a conflict of interest. A conflict of interest occurs when the inside information about one client could be given to another client or used for another client's benefit. You must never get yourself into any situation that appears to be a conflict of interest.

Conflicts can easily occur when you are working with more than one client. As a freelancer, you get the inside scoop, and often know what the client is doing or planning. Many times, it is your job to work on the new project, getting copy, press kits, or product brochures ready for release. This inside information is just that: information that your client wants kept under wrap until a specific release date. You cannot breach your client's trust by deliberately or inadvertently releasing the information to anyone.

It is common for some clients to request a nondisclosure agreement from the freelancer. The more competitive the business of the client, the more likely you will be asked to execute one. Often several pages in length, the agreement binds you not to release any information you learn from working with the client. The agreement varies from client and locale. Some are quite involved, and others are generic and simple-to-read documents.

If you work on retainer, doing PR writing, for example, clients may request you avoid working for any other buisness in the field. This doesn't avoid all conflicts—a banking client may have products similar to an insurance client's, but it does simplify things.

Avoid the Conflict

Whenever you think you might have a potential conflict of interest, resolve it immediately. The fastest way to eliminate any problem is to ask your current client if he believes it is a conflict. Your client will tell you if it is or isn't. If it is, you must turn down the assignment from the new client (even if you have the potential to make much more money). You must always act only in your client's best interest.

Some examples of potential conflicts of interest follow:

1. You have done design work for Advertising Agency A. Advertising Agency B wants you to do similar work. Because you have learned about the clients of Advertising Agency A, you should not accept work from Advertising Agency B.

2. You wrote an article for *Brides Magazine*. You cannot write a similar article for *Today's Weddings*.

3. You have created a press kit about the soon-to-be-released, super GPS receiver for XYZ Manufacturing. ABC Products wants you to write a product brochures about its new GPS systems to be released later this year.

In each of the previous examples, you have inside knowledge that could hurt your client if you work with its competitor. In the following examples, there is probably not any conflict of interest:

1. You are teaching a course at the local community college about writing press releases. Employees from both Client A and Client B are members of the class.

2. You are writing resumes for job seekers, knowing that the resumes will be sent to both Client A and Client B.

Interests that Conflict

Whether you signed a nondisclosure agreement or not, it is just not worth it to get yourself into a conflict of interest situation. Being sued might be the least of your problems. Your best and easiest way is to avoid conflicts? When you have a question in your mind, ask your current client if he sees a conflict. If he does, avoid taking on the other assignment from the other potential client. Being forthright can only improve your standing with your client.

3. You are writing a magazine article about pretzel making. One article is presented to a food magazine, while another similar but different article is proposed to a travel publication.

Plagiarism

Clients demand—and expect—that your work be original, not copied from another source. Abusing that expectation is tempting and easy today with the internet and the Copy command on a computer. A few quick mouse clicks, and mounds of copied information can be cobbled together. You could turn it in for a quick paycheck. But that is not what clients want.

Clients want fresh, original content. They certainly do not want to hire a freelancer and have that freelancer turn in plagiarized material. Clients that use plagiarized or unauthorized copied material are open to lawsuits and embarrassing publicity.

As a freelancer, never plagiarize or use unauthorized material as part of any assignment. Many times permission to quote a portion of someone's material can be easily gained just by asking. Some owners of material require the payment of a usage fee, while others grant permission to use the material without any fee. If you cannot obtain permission to use the materials that others have created, never use them.

Dealing with Clients

Clients expect their freelancers to be ethical, honest, and loyal. You should never propose to do something improper or accept an improper proposal. It never works out for the freelancer. Any client that would want you to do something illicit is not the kind of client that you want. Most clients assume that if you are willing to do something improper for them, you would also do the same sort of improper thing against them. Their solution is to sever ties with you.

Even though you might be thinking you are helping by following a client's illegal request, you are on treacherous ground. The solution is simple: never do anything that a client might perceive to be improper or disloyal. Strive to keep your client's interests above yours, and your loyalty will be recognized and rewarded by your client with a continued, long-term working relationship.

Professional Conduct

No matter what type of freelancing you are doing, you must always be a professional. Many professional organizations have developed a code of ethics that its members pledge to abide by. For example, the Society of Professional Journalists, a professional society that promotes the highest standards in journalism, adopted a code of ethics. One small part of the code states, "Journalists should test the accuracy of information from all sources and exercise care to avoid inadvertent error. Deliberate distortion is never permissible." This only makes sense. As a freelance journalist, you should only report accurate facts to your readers.

As a freelancer, when you are a member of a professional association or society you should strive to abide by its code of ethics. By doing so, you are raising your own professional conduct. In other words, if you follow the code of ethics, you are not likely to damage your relationship with any client. Although you can work in your pajamas or your shorts, T-shirt or sweatsuit, you must always be professional. Never let your client see you as anything other than a professional.

Spelling Rules

This is a simple yet an important rule. You cannot break this rule. When it comes to spelling, don't guess. If you don't know how to spell the word, look it up. All freelancers should have dictionaries within reach in their work area. Don't depend on your word processor to find all your typos or spelling errors. Consider this simple example:

> Dear Mr. Deer,
> Thank you for writing about your new John Deere tractor.

Your word processor would find nothing wrong with the example being spelled as:

> Deere Mr. Dear,
> Thank you for writing about your new John Deer tractor.

Yet it is wrong. And it may be wrong because computer dictionaries do not agree with the dictionaries most writers use—or should use. Microsoft Word may accept "non-profit," but *Webster's Dictionary* doesn't. Always check your spelling.

Your Never List

As a nonfiction writer, you must never do some things. These acts not only hurt your income, but can destroy your nonfiction writing career. This is called "Your Never List:"

○ *Never miss a deadline!* Think about the word *deadline*. Two simple words, placed neatly together. Cross the line, and you are dead! And you sure do not want to be dead. Always meet your deadlines, no matter what it takes.

○ *Never allow anyone to review and alter your work before it is published* (other than your editor).

○ *Never compromise yourself.* Avoid situations where you might feel pressured or tempted to write something that is not true. A good example might be that someone offers you a free trip to a beach resort for three days. Now you must write a good review, and overlook the high food and beverage prices the resort charges. Your integrity as a nonfiction writer is more important than any bribe or freebie that you might receive.

○ *Never get into a position of a conflict of interest.* You cannot write the same article for two competing publications, especially when you have received inside information from one of the two publications.

○ *Never fake or make up facts.* A nonfiction writer's job is to report the truth, good or bad. Never fake a source, fact, or interview.

○ *Never be unethical in dealing with editors, publishers, or people you are interviewing.*

○ *Never plagiarize.*

Marketing
Yourself via
Query Letters

Writing simple correspondence should be easy for a freelance writer. But for some reason, many writers, particularly beginners, struggle with the concept. People who have prepared beautifully written manuscripts— obviously talented at creating the written word—struggle enormously when they attempt to write a simple one-page letter to the person that has the power to get them published.

Because writing a query letter is so scary to many freelancers, the bloodcurdling task is put off and ignored. It is almost as if the writer wishes the query would magically write itself. Hopeful thinking like that still does not produce the anxiety-laden query.

Some freelancers become successful more quickly than others. Freelancers with less ability, fewer skills, and less education may excel at

> **Bright Idea**
> You can use the same principles for querying publishers to other businesses. You can query non-profit associations, advertising agencies, PR firms, and other potential marketing targets. Query submission is simply a specialized form of direct marketing.

the freelancing game, while talented freelancers find little work. The ability to prepare an effective query letter directly connects to the level of success of a freelancer. It is nothing more than pitching an idea and hoping a potential client becomes your customer. Not all will say yes—but some will.

In publishing, editors quickly get swamped with inappropriate manuscripts. Writers, so desperate for publication, send a barrage of drivel, throwing their misdirected manuscripts at anyone, hoping someone wants to publish it. It does not take long for most editors to stop looking at unsolicited manuscripts. The only way to break into publication is to write a coherent, well-thought-out query letter.

Don't waste precious time in your career by not learning how to master the simple techniques it takes to write an effective query letter. Read, study, and learn the skills offered in this book. Remember, you must market yourself. Query letters market you and your work idea to someone that needs freelancers but does not know about you, your work, or your talents. In other words, you are saying, "Here I am! I am great, wonderful, and I want to work for you!"

Queries for All Freelancers

All freelancers must know how to write an effective query letter. It does not matter what type of freelancing you plan to pursue. Eventually, you will need to write letters to an unknown editor, potential client, or person that could hire you to work as a freelance writer. The reception your query receives determines if a publisher accepts or rejects your writing for publication.

Effective query letters benefit both client and freelancer. Potential clients, such as editors, prefer to review a one-page letter rather than a ten-page manuscript. Freelancers also receive a faster response from an editor by using a query.

Nonfiction Writing

Nonfiction writers working magazine markets produce the most queries. They use query letters extensively to interest an editor in their proposed article. (The same technique used to sell to magazine editors can be used by just about any freelancer seeking work from any potential client.) Magazine editors prefer receiving a query rather than a completed manuscript.

They rarely read, much less publish, an unsolicited manuscript. When received in the editorial office, unsolicited manuscripts are tossed on a pile affectionately known as the slush pile. There the manuscript sits, among the many others. When there is spare time, someone, usually very junior, skims through books in the slush pile. The reader rejects most, stuffing them into the enclosed self-addressed, stamped envelope (SASE). If there is no SASE enclosed, he tosses the manuscript into the trash can.

An editor may publish a manuscript that was found in the slush pile, but it is a rare occurrence. Most editors say that they use manuscripts discovered in their slush pile once every two to three years.

A query letter allows the editor to add input into the creation of the article. By querying first (rather than sending a completed manuscript), you are giving the editor a chance to provide feedback on your idea. Editors often suggest a preferred article length or a specific approach to the piece. The editor may have additional research sources to give you, or may recommend people or experts to interview. By finding out what the editor wants in the finished article before you start writing, you are avoiding a later revision.

> **Dollar Stretcher**
>
> Don't include a SASE for nonpublisher queries. For example, if you are sending a query to an ad agency or a PR firm, there is no need to include a SASE.

Another advantage of submitting a well-written query to an editor is that it can result in future assignments. If the editor is impressed by your style and credentials, but does not want your current idea, she might suggest or offer another assignment. A well-written, professional query is often the beginning of a long, mutually beneficial relationship between an editor and a writer.

Agent Hunting

Many writers seek the assistance of a literary agent during their writing careers. Agents are primarily used to sell book manuscripts or screenplays. The writer, either fiction or nonfiction, uses a query letter to solicit the services of the literary agent. The query sells the agent on both the concept of the project and the ability of the writer. Few agents today look at unsolicited manuscripts. Most prefer a query letter as the first contact from the potential client.

Writer versus Editor

Many writers think of editors as their enemies rather than as their allies. It is warfare: Writer versus Editor. Editors are not the evil devils so many writers believe them to be. It's just that a big part of an editor's job is to say no. A book editor, for example, must say no to many writers. Suppose that as the publisher's acquisitions editor, the maximum number of books accepted and published this year is to be 30. If the editor has signed all 30, the next writer inquiring receives a no. It is not personal. It is just business. It has nothing to do with the editor. It is just part of the job.

The same is true for a fiction editor in a magazine. If he only buys two pieces of fiction for each magazine and he has already bought enough manuscripts for the next year, you will receive a no from the editor. It does not mean you are a bad writer or have a terrible idea, it means, once again, that the editor is just doing his job.

As a freelance, you must expect editors or potential clients to say no to you. It is as much a part of your job as a writer as it is of their jobs as editors or gatekeepers. The no is not what you want to hear, but you should realize that it often has nothing to do with your value as a writer or freelancer, or your idea. It is more often than not a business decision.

Writers often badmouth editors for the editing their work received under the editor's hand. This issue is out of the scope of the topic of this book, but this kind of thing does happen from time to time. If you, as a writer, cannot stand to have your work edited (and yes, sometimes butchered in the process), you may have chosen the wrong profession.

So far, this discussion involves the negativity associated with editors by writers. But editors are not a bunch of cold-hearted individuals that only say no. Many times, they do not say no. They instead say yes. Remember that every nonfiction article published and every book released started with a query letter. Editors do say yes. It happens every day. It is your job as a writer to get an editor to say yes to you. Developing your skill in preparing effective query letters increases your chances of receiving that yes.

Your First Test

The query letter you send is your first test. By it and it alone, you will be judged. Whether it is being read by the editor-in-chief, an editorial assistant, or a literary agent, an opinion will be formed about you as a writer. A well-written query proves to an editor that you are qualified to write the piece, that you are a professional.

The first question your query must answer is, "Can this writer communicate effectively?" If your query contains grammatical errors, spelling mistakes, or rambling, incoherent sentences, you will be considered sloppy and someone to avoid.

Your query also demonstrates to the reader how well your idea is refined and if it is something they might consider for publication. The quality of your idea development is another part of this first test. Pass it, or you will receive your rejection.

To be successful, your query must past this first test. Its readers in the publisher's or agent's office will be putting it (and you) to that test. Know, too, that they receive hundreds of queries per week, and they have plenty with which to compare your query. It is up to you to prove that you have a basic grasp of grammar and spelling, and that you can express your idea in a comprehensive, contemporary manner.

Of course, the other part of the test is how well your idea fits into the overall goals of the publisher. If your idea is about how to housebreak a puppy, it is unlikely that idea will have any relevance to a fashion magazine editor, no matter how well communicated.

It is often easier for the readers in the publisher's or agent's office to reject your query than it is to say yes. As they sit there, working their way through a pile of query letters, without doubt a stack of rejection forms is within arm's reach. As your query is read, it is easy to reach for the rejection slip, and send you that rejection. Your query has been handled. If you give them a reason to say no, they will say just that.

The work begins, for the editor or literary agent, when they say yes. Now they have to look at your work, decide if it is good enough for their publishing plans, and negotiate with you, work with you, and actually publish your writing. So it is easier to say no. But they cannot say no to everyone. If they did, there would be no publishing. And if they do not publish, they are soon out of work.

So they want to say yes. Even if it does mean more work. But you can expect a no if you give them any reason to reject you. If you don't, then you get the answer you want. A well thought-out query and a professional approach is all it takes to get that yes.

What Is an Effective Query?

An effective query letter is one that works. There is no magic blueprint, no secret answer. There is no special formula for you. Nothing exists that will guarantee your total success. However, there are some points to consider when you begin to write query letters. The number-one rule is that you must complete it and send it out. It seems so simple, but it is one thing that so many writers do not finish. For some reason, they hold on to the query.

The only way to test the effectiveness of any query letter you write is to send it. You have to place it in the mail and get it in front of the editor. The effectiveness is tested when the editor responds. If you get a yes, then you have a created a perfect query letter.

Query writing is an art, not a science. There are rules to follow, tips, advice, and information. As a writer, you put this all together, and you write your queries. For the cost of a postage stamp, you get to place your idea in front of an editor. The response you receive tells you if you have written an effective query.

As with any other writing, the more query letters you write, the better your letters will become. It takes practice and a desire to keep trying. The rest of it is not that difficult. But you never give up! You keep trying. And you send out what you create. That is how all successful writers test the effectiveness of their queries.

Query Basics

All businesses generate sales. Without making sales, there is no business. Customers are the most important part of any business, and it works the same way in freelancing. As you have learned, freelancers are operating a small business. The business consists of providing freelancing services. Their customers are often publishers (and, of course, their readers). Successful freelancers must sell their services to their primary customers, which are the publishers.

Publishers hire people to assist them in the publishing process. Insofar as freelancers are concerned, the primary people in the publisher's office are editors. They are employees of the publisher designated to choose manuscripts for publication. Editors are the people to whom you must sell your services. They are the decision makers and the people that make the purchase from you.

It is possible for you to hire a salesperson to visit a publisher's office in an attempt to sell your writing services. Various sources say that sending a salesperson on a sales call can cost between $50 and $100 per call. This is not an economically feasible approach to selling your writing services to a publisher's editor.

You can also create your own salesforce and call on as many publishers as you want for a grand total of 82 cents per call. (Current U.S. first class postage is 41 cents. One stamp out,

Smart Tip Tip...

For many writers, creating query letters is not much fun. They think that writing query letters is a chore. As your competition, it is good for other writers to ignore the task. For you, it is best to master the craft, taking all the time necessary until you can produce effective query letters quickly and efficiently.

one stamp for your SASE) We call this mighty yet inexpensive salesforce of yours "query letters." This method is what you use to sell your services. It is an inexpensive yet effective method.

Mastering Query Letters

To be a successful freelancer, you must master the techniques of writing a query letter. This is your top priority. (The fact that you are reading this book is a good step toward mastering the skill of writing query letters.) This is your source of sales. Without sales, you have no writing business. With no writing business, you have no income.

Writing query letters is not as bad as it might seem. It is a matter of developing a specific writing skill. It is not difficult to master. As long as you intend to be a writer, you will be writing query letters.

Marketing and Query Letters

Query letters are your salesforce. They are the main source of marketing. There are other ways to market your services, but nothing will be as effective as a well-crafted query letter.

You may discover older freelance writers that never use a query letter. Instead, they simply prepare the complete manuscript, and then send it to publishers. This is not good advice. First, most writing markets want a query, not complete manuscripts. Second, almost all nonfiction editors want to give some input into your proposed piece. Third, you could spend a lot of time creating manuscripts that never sell. This probably affects nonfiction writers more than fiction writers, but if you want to make repeated sales, it does not make sense to do all the work of writing a complete article, only to get it rejected.

It makes far more sense to write only what is likely to be sold. It does not make sense to take the time to write a 2,500-word article and only hope that it sells. The editor may like the idea, but not the approach. The editor could want the article, but written in a different format. The editor might want several things added

Beware!

When an editor receives a complete, unsolicited manuscript from an unknown writer, the first thing the editor thinks is, "This was rejected from another publication." The editor will automatically think, "Why should I want something that someone else does not want?" They will look for a reason to reject rather than give your work a fair, sympathetic reading and appraisal of its worth.

that you never thought of when you proposed the article.

For all these reasons, it is best to sell by query. That is, do just enough research to know about your subject, and then query. Wait for a positive response before you write the entire manuscript. Use your time to develop queries and market the idea of your next piece.

> **Tip...**
>
> **Smart Tip**
> Never write a nonfiction manuscript that has not first been pre-sold via a query letter. Writing unsold manuscripts is just a way not to earn money for your work.

Developing Great Queries

Your query letter must sparkle and shine. You have only a few seconds to make a good first impression. Then you can never make a first impression again.

First Things First

Your query must follow the rules. Do you remember your seventh grade geography class? Do you remember how the teacher gave you outlines of maps, and you had to use the colored pencils to fill in different countries? The teacher made you label each one. If you did not do it the exact way the teacher said, you got a zero on your assignment. You had to follow the rules.

The same thing goes with query letters. You have to follow the rules. You get a zero, a rejection, if you don't.

Here is a list of the simple rules of writing query letters:

- Make your letter look clean and professional.
- Use standard 8.5-by-11-inch white paper.
- Print and format the letter neatly.
- Single-space the letter (in contrast with the double spacing required of manuscripts and proposals), with double space between paragraphs.
- Use 10 to 12 point standard black fonts, such as Times New Roman, Arial, or Courier. Avoid fancy fonts. Just because your computer and printer can make them, do not use them.
- Have no spelling errors and no typos.
- Have no grammatical errors.
- Make sure the letter is properly punctuated.
- Use a standard block format; it is easiest to set up and use.

The Five Elements

In addition to the basics of appearance, your query should consist of five simple parts:

1. Opener/teaser
2. Background
3. Story plan
4. Freelancer information
5. Close

Each of these sections is discussed below in more detail. If you are not writing a query letter to an editor or publishing professional, but rather to a local business proposing a project, use this same outline procedure to develop your query. Instead of a story plan, propose your project.

Opener/Teaser

The opener, or teaser, is the most important part of your query letter. Here is where you must sell your idea. It should be about 25 to 50 words long and a maximum of two or three sentences in length. It must be strong, engaging, and hook the reader. The more ho-hum it is, the more likely the rejection. The stronger the opening paragraph is, the more likely the reader will continue to the next section of the query letter.

Examples of good opener are:

- Ben Johnson was working in his dark laboratory. As he peered over his glasses that slid far down his nose, the stench was sickening. The smell of death was everywhere.

- Despite an appearance of being a normal, middle-class American family, something was terribly wrong in the Jackson household. Mary's thick coating of makeup would not hide the bruises anymore.

- "I never expected to get into drugs," Fred Smith says.

Smart Tip

Never start the hook with the words, "Would you be interested in reading an article about …"

In those three examples, the reader will probably want to know more. Is he likely to throw down the letter, or read on? Has his interest been piqued? If the answer is yes, it is a successful opener.

Background

The next section, the second paragraph of the query, is the background information. After engaging the reader, here you begin to explain a bit more about the subject of your proposed piece.

This can be longer than the teaser.

Story Plan

This is your third paragraph. Here you tell the editor how you intend to approach your subject, the manner in which you plan the piece. By now, the editor either loves your idea or hates it. If he's reading onto the next section, you are close to getting a go-ahead.

Freelancer Information

The fourth part of the query letter is where you sell yourself as a writer. Here is where you list your credits and the reasons why you should be writing the proposed article.

Close

In this final section of the query letter, you close the letter, extending a standard business thank you for consideration.

Putting the Five Elements Together

Now it is just a matter of putting these five elements together. Your letter needs to be:

- Clear
- Brief
- Persuasive
- Interesting
- Specific
- Original

And never forget that it, as well as you, must always be professional.

What You Never Say in a Query

You never say some things in a query letter. Before developing your style, keep these thoughts in mind:

- Do not discuss any price or payment.
- Never tell the editor of your inexperience.
- Never mention that the proposed piece has been rejected elsewhere.

- Do not use hyperbole.
- Do not mention how long and hard you have been working on this article.
- Never state the piece needs more work.
- Never ask for help, advice, critiques, comments, or assistance.
- Never say that it would be thrilling to be published in the editor's publication.
- Do not discuss business in a query letter, or rights, payments, copyright registrations, or other similar issues.
- Never make threats or assertions to the potential client or editor, such as if you do not hear from the editor within two weeks, you will submit the idea elsewhere.
- Do not ask for a meeting or a lunch date.
- Never ask for advice on who else might like this wonderful idea, if the editor rejects it.
- Do not put extras in your envelope.
- Do not use any envelope other than a standard number-10 white business envelope.
- Do not beg or plead.
- Do not offer opinions. For example, if you are proposing a profile piece on a nationally recognized celebrity, your personal opinion makes no difference. You must wear your journalistic hat and act as an impartial reporter.
- Do not be cute.
- Avoid flamboyant stationery or perfumed paper.
- Do not mark the envelope "personal" in an attempt to avoid an editorial assistant.
- Never tell an editor what others think of your idea.
- Never trust any marketing list as the top resource for editors' names. It is best to do your own research using a reliable source.

Beware!

Never address a query letter, "To Whom It May Concern." Always get the editor's correct name and title, and double check the spelling of the editor's name.

Smart Tip

Never send a query letter without your phone number included. Many potential clients will use the telephone to contact you.

The Self-Addressed, Stamped Envelope

Every query letter should include a self-addressed, stamped envelope (SASE) if it is going to an editorial office. The courtesy of submitting an SASE proves you are a professional writer. If the editor chooses, your query and SASE might be returned on the editor's postage. But that decision should be left to the editor. In other than publishing businesses, the SASE is not necessary. For example, if you are pitching to a local public relations firm, send your query letter without enclosing the SASE.

Some self-addressed, stamped envelopes are never used or returned. What happens to them remains a mystery, and it is frustrating. That is just part of the business of being a writer. Get used to it, because it will happen to you.

Envelope to Use

You have two choices in envelopes for a SASE. You can use either a number-10 envelope, which you fold in thirds, or a number-9 envelope, which will slide flat inside a number-10 without being folded.

The SASE should be white. The postage stamp should be affixed. Your address should be placed on the envelope. You can use a rubber stamp, labels, or your printer to place your name and address on the envelope. Do not handwrite the SASE.

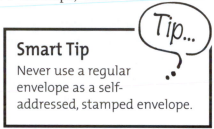

Smart Tip
Never use a regular envelope as a self-addressed, stamped envelope.

Postage Stamps

Be conservative with your postage stamps. It is best to use the standard, American flag stamps, always available at the post office. They help you maintain that professional image.

Use Imprinted Stationery to Improve Sales

If you are serious about being a freelancer, you should invest in imprinted stationery. It will cost about $200 for an initial supply of letterheads and envelopes. But that is a small price to pay when you see the results. You are announcing to the world (and to the editors and potential clients to whom you write) that you are a professional freelancer. You take your craft seriously. You are in business, and you intend to remain in business. Also, many of your competitors—other freelancers—do not bother to make this simple investment, so you stand out.

When buying printing services, buy what you want, not what the printer wants to sell you. Remember that printers are in business to sell printing. Do not let them talk you into colored or tinted papers, expensive parchments, or fancy designs. Use imprinted stationery that looks like it came from an attorney. If a lawyer would not use the stationery, you should not either. Choose a small, professional-looking typestyle design.

Of course, your name, address, phone number, e-mail address, and web site should be imprinted on the letterhead. If you have a fax number, you should include it. You might also want to include any professional organizations to which you belong. But that is it. Do not add descriptive words like writer, freelancer, or author.

Before You Get Imprinted Stationery

Until your budget permits the purchase of imprinted stationary, use your computer software to create a letterhead at the top of your page. It should be centered in the header area and include your name, address, phone number, and e-mail address.

Make sure you create the letterhead with an easily readable typeface. See the examples below for ideas.

This method of creating a letterhead is better than placing your name, address, and contact information under your signature.

The Proper Letterhead Style example is of a computer generated letterhead.

The Improper Letterhead Style example of a computer generated letterhead with a type style that should be avoided. Just because you have fancy fonts doesn't mean this is a good time to use them.

Proper Letterhead Style

George Sheldon

123 Main Street • Philadelphia, PA 19101

215-345-9999 • Fax: 215-999-9543

E-mail: george@anyemailplace.com

Improper Letterhead Style

George Sheldon

123 Main Street • Philadelphia, PA 19101

215-345-9999 • Fax: 215-999-9543

E-mail: george@anyemailplace.com

A Good Query

Now that you know the breakdown of a query letter and what not to do, it is time to assemble a good one. In this section we will build a query letter. Here are some assumptions:

- You are a freelance writer specializing in science and technology.
- You have learned about a local forensic scientist that developed a technique for collecting fingerprints from a corpse.
- You have never worked for the target market.
- You are new to this genre and have few credits.

Everything presented here is fiction, used only for training and education purposes. With those assumptions, let us build the query letter!

Step 1: Type the date, and the editor's name and information

December 21, 20XX

Alice Yesiam, Editor
Police Science Times
123 Main Street
Philadelphia, PA 19101

Dear Ms. Yesiam:

Step 2: Create the opener/teaser

Ben Johnson was working in his dark laboratory. As he peered over his glasses that slid far down his nose, the stench was sickening. The smell of death was everywhere.

Step 3: Write the background information

As a leading expert in latent fingerprints, Professor Johnson learned how to lift fingerprints from a corpse. Now a nationwide expert, police investigators throughout the country constantly seek the assistance of this Penn State professor. In today's mail deliveries was a FedEx pouch from the Las Vegas Police Department. Its contents included a grisly right hand from a murder victim. Professor Johnson smiled as he looked over the smelly remains under an intense ultraviolet light. "Bingo!" he said with a boyish glee.

Step 4: Suggest the story plan

I am preparing an article with the working title, "What Will Professor Johnson Find on Your Corpse?" Approximately 1,500 words in length, my article will profile the professor, and discuss his unique success in recovering latent fingerprints from cadavers. I would also include a side-bar that fully informs the reader of the technique Professor Johnson developed.

Step 5: Sell yourself as the writer

Please respond with confidence, as I am a full-time freelance writer with numerous writing credits in such publications as *Popular Mechanics*, *Decision*, and *Pennsylvania*. I am a member of the National Writers Union.

Step 6: Close the letter

Thank you for your consideration. I have enclosed a self-addressed, stamped envelope for your reply. I will look forward to hearing from you.

And there it is. A query letter prepared following simple guidelines. The pieces are put together in the formatted Sample Query Letter on page 66.

> **Tip...**
>
> **Smart Tip**
> Keep your query letters short! Never exceed one page.

Additional Comments about the Sample Query

Is this a perfect query? Not yet. One more thing that absolutely must be done is so simple, yet so many fail to do it. And it is an absolute necessity. You must send it out! It will only be judged perfect if:

1. It is sent out, and
2. The editor bites and wants the piece.

Once the editor says yes to the pitch or idea, then it is perfect. No one can argue that. The goal of the query has been achieved: It sold the idea, and the editor said yes to you as the writer.

Really A. Writer

987 North Second Street • Harrisburg, PA 17101

717-989-9889 • Fax: 717-989-9880 • E-mail: raw@internet.com

December 21, 20XX

Alice Yesiam, Editor

Police Science Times

123 Main Street

Philadelphia, PA 19101

Dear Ms. Yesiam:

Ben Johnson was working in his dark laboratory. As he peered over his glasses that slid far down his nose, the stench was sickening. The smell of death was everywhere.

As a leading expert in latent fingerprints, Professor Johnson learned how to lift fingerprints from a corpse. Now a nationwide expert, police investigators throughout the country constantly seek the assistance of this Penn State professor. In today's mail deliveries was a FedEx pouch from the Las Vegas Police Department. Its contents included a grisly right hand from a murder victim. Professor Johnson smiled as he looked over the smelly remains under an intense ultraviolet light. "Bingo!" he said with a boyish glee.

I am preparing an article with the working title, "What Will Professor Johnson Find on Your Corpse?" Approximately 1,500 words in length, my article will profile the professor, and discuss his unique success in recovering latent fingerprints from cadavers. I would also include a sidebar that fully informs the reader of the technique Professor Johnson developed.

Please respond with confidence, as I am full-time freelance writer with numerous writing credits in such publications as *Popular Mechanics*, *Decision*, and *Pennsylvania*. I am a member of the National Writers Union.

Thank you for your consideration. I have enclosed a self-addressed, stamped envelope for your reply. I will look forward to hearing from you.

Sincerely,

Really A. Writer

Really A. Writer

Could the letter be improved? Yes. I would suggest that the writer offer some advice about photographs or art to the editor. I would also suggest adding how long the writer thinks the sidebar might be.

Smart Tip

Tip...

Always suggest a sidebar! Editors love them. Most nonfiction writers ignore them. They give you an opportunity to write a longer piece, and thus earn more money.

The Guarantee

There is one more thing that will *improve* this query letter and increase the chances of the editor saying yes. It is your throwing in a guarantee that the editor cannot refuse because it diminishes her risk. An editor is always reluctant to waste time or money on an unknown freelance writer. Every editor has been burned more than once by a writer. So it is easier to say no than to have a problem with a writer. If the article comes in and is, in plain words, lousy, the editor knows the writer still wants to be paid. At best, the editor will spend money on a kill fee, which is paying the writer to go away. Eliminate this problem by adding this line at the end of your query:

> If you are interested in this article, I will be happy to complete the article purely upon speculation.

This is an extremely powerful statement. Now the editor has nothing to lose. If the editor is only mildly interested in your idea, this could get you a yes rather than no.

Agreeing to work on speculation means that if you blow the assignment, you get paid nothing. If the editor likes your piece, you made your sale. You can use this method to break into more editorial offices and publications than you can imagine, few writers use this technique. The writers that I have taught to use this have done extremely well by adding this line to their query letters. Once the editor knows your work, drop this offer.

The Slant

Every article, story, and publication has a slant. Let's consider someone you have heard something about: Rush Limbaugh. Rush is a conservative radio talk show host and is controversial. Those who listen to his show soon develop an opinion about him.

Let us suppose that you want to write a profile about Rush. No matter what, you would have to slant the article one way or the other. For example, Rush is the greatest radio talk show host ever, or Rush is the worst radio talk show host ever. One way or the other, your article would need to be slanted.

The way you slant your writing will certainly influence your writing career, and your income. All publishers have a blind spot although it is something they do not want to talk about or even acknowledge that might exist. Think about those free in-flight magazines published by the major airlines. Do you think they would ever admit in print that an airplane crashes? That is their blind spot. *Running Magazine* will never admit that running is a dumb sport and people that do it are insane, especially if they do it in 12-degree weather with a wind chill that makes it feel like minus 17 degrees. A liberal political magazine would never admit Rush is right about anything, and a conservative publication would never admit that Bill Clinton did one thing right while he was president.

So it is important for you to learn what a magazine's slant is and how to write a slanted article. It is an expression of a specific point of view. With Rush Limbaugh, for example, two distinct articles could be written about him. You should not just write an editor and ask if they are interested in a piece about Limbaugh without including your slant. Tell the editor about your planned approach or slant in your query. It belongs in the story plan section of the query letter.

Writing Style

With some experience and time, you can develop a favorable, congenial writing style in your query and cover letters. The overall point you should remember is that your query letters should be friendly, but businesslike. You have to prove you can deliver not only a great writing product but also do so with flair and style. It might help to remember that you are writing a query to an editor, an individual person, and not to a large audience. Your query should be a one-on-one letter from a writer to an editor. Try to keep your letters from being stuffy and boring by an overuse of business language. A slight tone of informality is the ultimate goal.

Your writing in a query letter should be concise. If you can say it in two words rather than three, do so. This may take some time to develop. But it should be a goal you want to achieve.

Marketing Yourself via Fax or E-Mail

Sooner or later, you will think, "I can market my freelancing services by sending e-mails or faxes." What sounds like a great idea, and a cost-effective, efficient method, is fraught with problems.

The days of mass marketing by e-mail and fax are gone. Today, the general rules are simple: if a prospect asks for information, you can deliver it via e-mail or fax. If you have an ongoing business relationship, you can probably market to that person via either e-mail or fax, but you'd be better off to seek permission before doing so. You cannot, however, just create and send unsolicited e-mail or faxes to potential prospects or clients.

Unsolicited Faxing Prohibited

The Telephone Consumer Protection Act (TCPA) of 1991 prohibited using a telephone facsimile (fax) machine, computer, or other device to send an unsolicited advertisement, or *"junk fax,"* to a fax machine. The Federal Communications Commission (FCC) enforces laws against junk faxing. In so doing, the FCC has issued public information about sending unsolicited commercial faxes. In general, the TCPA and the FCC rules prohibit most unsolicited facsimile (fax) advertisements.

Congress also passed the Junk Fax Prevention Act in 2005. The law directs the FCC to amend its rules adopted pursuant to the TCPA regarding fax advertising. According to the FCC, the revised rules are:

- codify an established business relationship (EBR) exemption to the prohibition on sending unsolicited fax advertisements;
- define EBR for unsolicited fax advertisements;
- require the sender of fax advertisements to provide specified notice and contact information on the fax that allows recipients to "opt-out" of any future faxes from the sender; and
- specify the circumstances under which a request to "opt-out" complies with the Act.

According to the FCC, to "understand the revised rules, you must first understand the meaning of the terms 'unsolicited advertisement' and 'established business relationship.'" As defined in FCC rules, an "unsolicited advertisement" is "any material advertising the commercial availability or quality of any property, goods, or services which is transmitted to any person without that person's prior express invitation or permission, in writing or otherwise.

> **Bright Idea**
> The FCC has all of its fax rules online. Get the latest information by visiting the FCC web site at www.fcc.gov.

Fax Broadcasters

There are companies that provide fax-broadcasting services. They will send a fax to your list, or to a list of fax numbers it has prepared. According to the FCC, you are responsible even if you hired a fax broadcasting company: "Generally, the person or

> **Beware!**
> Be careful with any fax broadcasting service you find on the internet. It is quite possible that an offer that looks too good is from a company located outside of the United States. You could be held liable for faxes they generate on your behalf.

business on whose behalf a fax is sent or whose property, goods, or services are advertised is liable for a violation of the junk fax rules, even if the person or business did not physically send the fax," the FCC says. "A fax broadcaster also may be liable if it has a high degree of involvement in the sender's fax message, such as supplying the fax numbers to which the message is sent, providing a source of fax numbers, making representations about the legality of faxing to those numbers, or advising about how to comply with the junk fax rules. Also, if a fax broadcaster is highly involved in the sender's fax messages, the fax broadcaster must provide its name on the fax."

Opt-Out Notice Requirements

The FCC requires opt-out notices on all faxes. According to the FCC, "Senders of permissible fax advertisements (those sent under an EBR or with the recipient's prior express permission) must provide notice and contact information on the fax that allows recipients to opt-out of future faxes. The notice must:

- be clear and conspicuous and on the first page of the advertisement;
- state that the recipient may make a request to the sender not to send any future faxes and that failure to comply with the request within 30 days is unlawful; and
- include a telephone number, fax number, and cost-free mechanism (including a toll-free telephone number, local number for local recipients, toll-free fax number, web site address, or e-mail address) to opt-out of faxes. These numbers and cost-free mechanism must permit consumers to make opt-out requests 24 hours a day, seven days a week. Senders who receive a request not to send further faxes that meets the requirements listed in the next section must honor that request within the shortest reasonable time from the date of the request, not to exceed 30 days. They are also prohibited from sending future fax advertisements to the recipient unless the recipient subsequently provides prior express permission to the sender."

Violations and Penalties

The FCC does issue warning citations and impose fines against companies violating or suspected of violating the junk fax rules, but it does not award individual damages. In addition to complaining to the FCC, an individual can file TCPA-related complaints with state authorities, including local or state consumer protection offices or the state attorney general's office.

Bulk e-mailing is also illegal. The CAN-SPAM Act of 2003 established requirements and penalties for those that send commercial e-mail. The Federal Trade Commission (FTC) enforces this law. The fines for violations are substantial, according to the FTC. "Each violation of the law's provisions is subject to fines of up to $11,000. Deceptive commercial e-mail also is subject to laws banning false or misleading advertising." Additional fines are provided for commercial e-mailers who not only violate the rules described above, but also:

Smart Tip

Don't even consider any scheme that would "mask" your e-mail. Getting caught doing so is just not worth it.

- "harvest" e-mail addresses from web sites or web services that have published a notice prohibiting the transfer of e-mail addresses for the purpose of sending e-mail.

- generate e-mail addresses using a "dictionary attack"—combining names, letters, or numbers into multiple permutations.

- use scripts or other automated ways to register for multiple e-mail or user accounts to send commercial e-mail.

- relay e-mails through a computer or network without permission, for example, by taking advantage of open relays or open proxies without authorization."

Querying via E-Mail

While you cannot bulk e-mail or spam potential clients or prospects, you can send a query. As discussed in Chapter 7, queries are a form of direct marketing that freelancers use to gain work.

A few years ago, editors, agents, and publishers did not accept e-mail queries. That is no longer the case in today's electronic world. Now e-mail addresses are a part of nearly every market listing in the various resources for writers. E-mail communication is part of the publishing world. Editors and writers are using e-mail, and the trend is one likely to grow.

Some editors and publishers still prefer the traditional paper query. If they do, do not intrude via e-mail. Send a letter via regular surface mail.

Electronic publications, such as web sites, e-zines, and e-mail newsletters, prefer and require electronic query. Many electronic publications will not even bother to consider paper queries. As with most technology, there are advantages and disadvantages. E-mail is no exception.

Advantages of Using E-Mail Queries

There are advantages to using e-mail queries over traditional paper queries. E-mail queries save money on postage. They are faster, reaching the editor's mailbox within seconds after you send them. Your reply, yes or no, from the editor moves at the same accelerated speed. It is possible to send a query and have a reply from the editor within minutes, rather than weeks.

Fun Fact

One editor of a trade publication based in New Jersey admitted that he "doesn't always see all of his e-mail." The reason: at the time he made the statement, he had over 14,000 e-mails in his inbox."

Disadvantages of Using E-Mail Queries

E-mail queries have disadvantages, too. E-mail, as it has developed over the years as a medium, has a tone of informality. Editors complain that e-mail queries seem to be prepared hastily or sloppily, as if not enough thought was put into the letter. E-mail queries often lack style, and the desired level of professionalism editors want to see in a query is lost. E-mail queries seem too casual or chatty to many editors. Writers turn to cute rather than remain businesslike. With e-mail, photocopied clips cannot be enclosed.

Editors also complain about writers' impatience when corresponding via e-mail. They say that just because a query arrives within seconds, it does not mean the editor is going to read it immediately. Editors seldom respond within minutes, and they become quickly annoyed by writers that begin nagging for a response within hours or days of sending an e-mail query.

Finally, e-mail may be automatically blocked because of spam-blocking software. Your e-mail may not make it to editor's mailbox.

Tip...

Smart Tip
Write your query letter in your word processing software. When completed, spell check, then copy and paste the letter into your e-mail software.

Other Considerations

Writers should make sure they are actually set up to send electronic queries. Most importantly, make sure your e-mail software is properly installed. Make sure your correct e-mail address is in the return section, so if an editor replies, he can send a message to you with little effort.

E-mail queries contain the same elements as traditional regular mail. The query should look like a regular mailed letter, with the addition of the elements of an e-mail correspondence. However, e-mail formatting is slightly different and the e-mail query, because of the nature of e-mail, has extra elements that must be considered, such as the header and signature box.

The Header

E-mail messages contain a header. The header provides vital identification information about you and your query. Be sure to put the right information in these sections:

- *To*: Always send your query to the right person at the right address. Avoid sending to a generic or group e-mail box, such as the editors@magazine.com. Locate the exact e-mail address of the editor. If it is not available, then send the query via regular mail.

- *From*: Make sure your correct name is included in this section of the header. If you have an online personality, such as "Dark Shadow," make sure that it is not showing up in your e-mails to an editor.

Smart Tip
Tip...
Avoid cuteness in your subject line. Informality, such as "May I have a moment of your time?" looks too much like spam or unsolicited commercial e-mail and could cause your query to be instantly deleted or ignored.

- *Subject*: Always start the subject section of the e-mail header with the word "Query," along with a brief description of your proposal. Some examples might be "Query—Travel to Pennsylvania" or "Query—Profile of Bruce Willis." Never leave the subject line blank.

Body of E-Mail Text

The best way to handle the text or body of an e-mail query is to assume it is a traditional query. Include the editor's name and address, just as you would if you were sending a traditional query. Include a date line. Write your e-mail query with a "Dear Mr. Howard" greeting. Follow all of the rules to make your query look professional and formal.

Bright Idea
When preparing an e-mail query, consider ways to condense your letter into a tight summary, allowing the editor to view your e-mail on a single screen with minimal scrolling.

Some editors have said that they prefer shorter queries by e-mail. This is often due to a computer screen display issue: the query should require minimal scrolling by the editor. Some writers are even sending briefer, one paragraph e-mail queries. The tease is eliminated. The writer just pitches the story and closes with her credentials. This approach may work with some editors, but should be used minimally.

The Signature Block

Your e-mail query should include a standard signature block. The signature block should include your name, address, telephone number, e-mail address, and web site, if any. This is the same information you would include in a letterhead. With e-mail, the format requires that you place this information at the end of your correspondence.

Avoid cute signature blocks. Do not use graphics, photographs, or other images. Forget the barking dogs, dancing pencils, pictures of your kids, smiley faces, and other icons, no matter how cute they are. Keep your signature block professional.

Formatting an E-Mail Query

There is not much that can be done to improve the standard format of an e-mail query. Some software programs, such as Microsoft Outlook® offer formatting features such as wallpaper or backgrounds and tints to enhance the appearance of e-mail. Avoid the temptation to make your e-mail less boring. Be careful that you do not do anything that might make your query harder to read.

Here are some guidelines to help you format an e-mail query:

- Always single-space your text.
- Add an extra space or return between paragraphs.
- Use a block style to create your paragraphs. Do not indent.
- Avoid formatting commands, such as bold, italics, or underlines.
- Use shorter paragraphs. Avoid long blocks of text.
- Use a standard, easily readable font. Choose either 10- or 12-point, Arial, Times Roman, or Courier fonts.
- Never use emoticons, such as :), the smiley face.
- Never use bullets in an e-mail query. (They seldom show up as bullets on the receiving end.)
- Never send any attachments with an e-mail query. If your e-mail program automatically sends v-cards or some other attachments, turn that feature off.
- Do not use any other special characters such as accents or tildes.
- Avoid using HTML or other special types of formatting.
- Do not include graphics.
- Do not use colors on your background.
- Do not use colors in your fonts.

E-Mail Clips

Handling the clips issue is challenging when sending a query via e-mail, but not impossible. You can include a line saying "clips are available." If requested by the editor, send them via regular mail or fax.

Another option is to include a link to a web site that holds your clips. Obviously, that link must be working and easy to use. Some editors will check the sites you list; others will not. You can also turn the clips into Adobe Reader® PDF files, and offer to send them via e-mail. Another option is to offer to e-mail a text file containing the clip information. A scanned copy turned into a graphic file, although large, is yet another option. Never just send a clip without first receiving the OK from the editor. And never send any attachment without first receiving the go-ahead.

Marketing Yourself in Other Ways

As a freelance writer, you will spend a great deal of your time looking for work. The process is simple. You will participate in activities that either

- encourage potential clients to contact you when they have work, or

- allow you to contact potential clients offering to complete work.

Either of these simple, basic strategies works. It is probably best to use a combination of both in your never-ending attempt to find clients and work.

How Clients Find You

As you learned earlier, in today's world, every freelancer needs a web site. Don't use free web site services that are available, such as your local internet service provider's free web space for personal or small business use. Your free web site address might be something like this: www.verizon.net/~vze2321t4. It makes far more sense businesswise to set up a domain, such as: www.georgesheldon.com, www.georgewrites.com, or www.philadelphiasportswriter.com.

Web domains are inexpensive to set up and maintain, so there's no reason to use a free site. When someone needs a freelancer in your area or with your expertise, they'll be able to find you via the World Wide Web by completing a search on the various search engines, such as Google, Yahoo!, and Microsoft Live Search.

Clients can also find you via the internet when your name is listed on web sites. Some sites are free, while others charge for listings or advertisements. As you learned earlier, don't overspend money on advertising, even here. Free listings or ads, such as those available on craigslist (www.craigslist.org), might be beneficial. Of course, any place you can post or announce your services at no cost could prove worthwhile.

Another popular way to have potential clients find you via the web is by purchasing classified advertising from the major search engines. Small ads, with a link to your web site, are displayed when someone searches for a particular word or phrase. For example, someone might type the words *freelance writer* in a search engine. Your small ad would be displayed during the search result.

You purchase your search engine classified ad by selecting key words, and you set how much you are willing to pay for them. If you want to pay for a display of the words *freelance writer*, you set up those words and how much you are willing to pay for the display of your ad. Some ads are displayed for as low as one cent, but popular words and phrases often cost $5, $10, or more to get displayed. You can set a daily ad budget to prevent runaway advertising costs. If you opt for this method of promotion, experiment with your advertisement. The ads are small, and only a few words can be displayed. You are likely to get better results by staying regional or local, even though as a freelancer you can work for anyone in the world. It may make sense to try to advertise your services as a Los Angeles business writer rather than a worldwide freelance travel writer. Keep a close eye on your daily budget, and don't buy more classified advertising on search engines than you can afford.

Some professional organizations have lists, but they are only open to members. To get listed, you must purchase a membership (usually for a year), and the application process can be lengthy, as it is for the American Society of Journalists and Authors (ASJA). Other organizations make membership as simple as completing an application and paying a membership fee. Keep in mind that memberships often include other benefits. Your listing in a membership roster can be just another form of advertising. Evaluate what it costs for you to be a member of any freelancing organization, especially if you are paying primarily to be listed.

Pressing the Flesh

One of the best ways to find work is by meeting a wide range of people—in person. It's simple, easy, effective, yet seldom used by many in the freelancing business. Meet people, introduce yourself, and get to know them as potential clients.

Go where these potential clients are. If you are seeking local businesspeople, attend chamber of commerce events or other meetings where representatives of local businesses gather. Local professional associations often have monthly meetings. For example, if you are seeking the business of building contractors, there is probably a meeting of the local building contractors association in a nearby community. Get to those meetings and meet the people there.

If you want to work for editors and publishers, get out of your office and meet your potential clients. Try to meet them in their offices. Plan a trip to their city and ask for a get-to-know-you meeting. Call or write and ask for ten-minute meetings so you can understand their current and future editorial needs. Most editors and publishers will give you a few minutes. Just don't ask for more. Remember, they are always looking for good freelancers. Be professional (appropriate dress, manner, etc.) when meeting any potential client.

Don't be afraid to ask for referrals. Many editors or clients know others who might need your services and will give you a referral, especially if they do not have any work for you at the moment.

Half the Work Is Finding the Work

Successful freelancers must spend a significant amount of their time looking for work. In the beginning of any freelance operation, it is not unusual to spend 50 to 75 percent of the total work time marketing and seeking work. As your freelance operation is established, the total time spent looking is less, perhaps scaling back to 20 percent of work hours, which is still one full day each week.

Freelancers who do not continuously seek work are often out of work for long gaps. The trick is to keep work flowing and to have multiple projects underway. By doing this, a freelancer's income can be balanced and maintained, so never overlook the importance of a steady work flow.

No matter what type of writing you are doing, build time into your schedule to market your services actively and consistently.

Who Needs You Now

A freelancer can often find work by searching web sites, market lists, and advertisements. Many people needing freelancers advertise for help. Some potential clients advertise for full-time help. This often indicates an immediate need, and one you can fill. Your approach can be something like, "I noticed your full-time help wanted advertisement. I thought I might be able to help you until you get a new person on board and working."

Always Marketing

Because part of your ongoing work as a freelancer is marketing yourself and your freelancing business, you need to launch and maintain an effective marketing plan. Then, you can maintain work and develop a steady stream of income. Your plan should include a mix of marketing ideas, from pitching ideas to publishers and editors to speaking to local groups and teaching at local colleges. This way you get a variety of clients, both near and far away. And a good mix of clients and work makes sense from a business standpoint.

Bright Idea

Be approachable whenever you speak, and always offer a free handout that includes your name, address, phone number, and e-mail address. Try to develop a handout that the audience might want to keep. For example, if you give a presentation about how to write effective customer service letters, develop a handout, "Ten Steps to Better Customer Service Letters."

Speaking

If you enjoy public speaking, offer to speak at local business clubs, service organizations, the chamber of commerce, employee meetings, and any other place where potential clients might be. Prepare an effective speech (another sample of the kind of work you can do) with a stimulating title. Then offer the speech to any group that might want to hear it. Libraries are often places that allow you to speak. Speaking engagements can generate free publicity and cost little. While it is not for everyone, those that don't mind public speaking and doing presentations find it an effective marketing tool.

Teaching

If you can teach adults, there are probably many opportunities for you to work in your community. Community colleges, recreation associations, libraries, and even some businesses offer courses and classes on any number of subjects.

Many of these opportunities only pay you a small hourly rate. Nevertheless, they are a great way to get into the community. The people in your class may become clients. For example, if you teach a course on giving better speeches, those in attendance are likely to give speeches regularly. They may want to hire a freelancer to write those speeches. While they probably do want to learn how to write their own speeches, the reality of tight schedules and not enough time means that they will at least sometimes hire this work out to reliable freelancers. During your classes, you might mention that when you are hired as a speechwriter, you "have found the most effective way to complete this is to . . . ." This subtle mention is often all it takes to find work and new clients.

Meetings

Attend meetings at the local chamber of commerce, other business organizations, and networking groups in your local area. Making contacts and networking can always help to expand your business. There are usually occasional mixers or time built into the meetings to allow you to exchange business cards and "meet and greet" others. Dress appropriately, and don't be bashful. Shake hands, and let others know what you do. Most people will be happy to meet you, and keep your card for future reference. Get their cards—and keep in touch.

Publish a Newsletter

Another fast way to build a clientele is to create and publish your own newsletter. Unlike junk mail, newsletters find their way onto potential clients' desks. This is especially true if your newsletter is professional and contains worthwhile information. Newsletters deemed to be of value are not tossed away but retained because of the information in them. A personal newsletter can be a pricy marketing tool, but if you have the budget to produce them on a regular basis, don't overlook this method of communication with current clients and prospects.

Write and Publish White Papers

White papers provide technical or detailed information. They are also a great way to develop another sample of what you can produce. Create your own white paper, and send it to potential clients. If there is value in the information, the white paper will probably be retained. The potential client then has your name and contact information neatly filed in his office.

Launch Your Own PR Campaign

As a freelancer, you might be called upon to be a part of, or run, a PR campaign. You can do the same thing for yourself by launching your own public relations campaign. Issue press releases, make news, and get your name out to the business community. Announce your freelance business, conduct surveys and publish results, or make news by doing something special in the community. And keep it up. Don't be a three news-release business: announcing your opening, moving to bigger quarters, and your closing.

Develop a database of local media, and work your list. Plan your campaigns with creativity and vigor. For example, plan to do something special for the local humane league during the dog days of summer. As you produce your PR campaign, you will develop important contacts in your local area.

Volunteer for a Nonprofit

Rather than sitting around and waiting for your phone to ring or your e-mail box to fill, get to work by volunteering for a local nonprofit. Your local chapter of the United Way, Make-a-Wish Foundation, American Red Cross, or Salvation Army, for example, will certainly appreciate any time you can devote to them. If you volunteer, get involved. Serve on a committee or two, and meet other local businesspeople. These connections can certainly pay off with ongoing work from new clients.

Finding Your First Customers

As you begin your freelance writing career, you might have to work for less pay when you do not have much experience in an area. Once you have some clips or samples—proof that you are a reliable freelancer that can get work done—more potential clients will be willing to work with you. Getting those first clips are important.

> **Fun Fact**
>
> A clip is a clipping or photocopy of an article you wrote. Your byline shows you are the writer of the piece. Once you have clips, you can prove that you are a published freelancer. You use those clips to get into other, more lucrative markets. In other words, use your clips as steppingstones.

Marketing via E-Mail or Legal Fax

As you have already learned in Chapter 8, you just can't spam or mass fax anyone. Although technology makes it easy to do, the law prohibits it. But you can use e-mail or faxes effectively and, most importantly, legally. The trick is to have potential prospects or clients request free, useful information from you. In the course of the signup process, offer to send additional information via e-mail or fax. You can market regularly to those that accept your offer. That way, you are not spamming them.

Say your primary target is claims managers of insurance companies. Among other services, your freelance service offers templates of well-written letters and staff training in which you teach how to write clear and concise correspondence. Now follow these steps:

1. *Develop a list of potential clients.* Your list would include all the insurance company claims managers in your service area.

2. *Create a document of interest to this group.* It should be something of value and something that would pique their interest. A white paper on the ten steps of improving business letter writing or a report on what insurance claims representatives need to know about writing claim denials are the kind of topics likely to get the attention of most claims managers.

3. *Send a letter offering the giveaway document for free.* Write a great pitch letter, and offer to give the document for free. To get a copy, invite the claims managers to log on to your web site to request their free copy.

4. *Ask if the requesters want a free monthly newsletter*. In the process of requesting your free document, include the offer of a free monthly newsletter via e-mail (or fax).

Those that say yes to your free offer have now consented to your regular publication, which will include a subtle marketing message. You could keep marketing by regular mail, sending out more letters. The downside to doing so is the postage expense. The prospects that consent to your e-mails are saving you the expense of printing and postage.

Bright Idea

Be sure to do a great job on the marketing project for your own service. You can use what you create as samples to show potential clients.

Specialization

versus

Generalization

As a freelance writer, you are offering to provide a service in the marketplace. You probably say that you will do anything the client needs or wants, but the reality is that not all freelance work is suitable for you. Nor are you suitable for all clients. Getting a hold on what you do and what you don't do is important for your long-term success. This requires you to decide if you are a specialist or a generalist.

What Are You Selling?

As you move toward opening your writing buisness, decide what it is that you are selling. Get more specific than writing or copyediting. Suppose, for example, your free-lancing business is one where you design web sites. There are different software and computer programs that are used to build a functional web site. A potential client contacts you and asks you to use a software product that you have never used, are unlikely to ever use again, and it would take you 40-hours of work just to learn the software. And the project is a database project, and something that has nothing to do with web sites.

Does it make sense to take on the assignment?

Probably not.

As a creative and intelligent freelancer, you probably could learn the software, and complete the project. An inexperienced freelancer might jump at the project. A more experienced freelancer will realize that it often makes sense to turn down work that is not a good fit for their business. Instead of getting bogged down in a quagmire, they spend their time looking for the kind of work they can do quickly, easily, and most importantly, profitably.

Specializing versus Generalizing

As a freelancer, one of your earliest business decisions is to decide if you are going to be a generalist or a specialist. Is it knowledge in depth on a few subjects or knowledge about a lot of topics that suits your personality and interests? There are advantages and disadvantages to each approach.

Advantages of Specialization

There are definite advantages to being a specialist. As a writer specializing in a particular area, assignments are easier to acquire. A specialist writing about topics he knows concentrates on just marketing and writing, and does not have to learn a new subject area.

Beware!

Many freelancers flounder because they do not resolve the issue of specialist or generalist. How you position yourself in the marketplace is how potential clients will see you. It can hurt or help your freelance business based on what you say you do or don't do.

Specializing allows you to establish a reputation as an expert in a field, which helps you achieve a higher income faster. If, for example, you are recognized as an expert about gardening, you may be sought after as a speaker or teacher, which allows you to expand your freelance business into other areas. Editors of publications will want your work, rejecting others for you, their recognized expert.

As you develop your level of expertise, your pay will increase from starting rates to the higher scales. If you specialize in one field, your clips will be on the same topics, making it easier to receive assignments. By specializing, you soon recognize what is news and what could be turned into a story or article for one of your stable of clients.

Your area of expertise must be in an area where you have passion. That passion turns into enthusiasm. If you do not care about the topic, there is little reason to specialize in it. You do not have to be a complete expert in any one field to be a specialist. There are plenty of things you won't know, but you will have a good idea where to look for the information you need.

Disadvantages of Specialization

There are several disadvantages to specialization. For one thing, it is easy to become too specialized. For example, let's say you own a dog, in particular, a boxer. You probably know something about the breed, having owned your boxer for a while. But would you want to specialize in writing about boxers? How many markets are there for this kind of information? *Dog Fancy* magazine may take an article, and perhaps you could find a dog book publisher that does not yet have a book about boxers. But the chances of making long-term, significant income from this writing specialty are small. Be careful not to be too much of a specialist.

Once you develop a specialty, you could have trouble switching to another kind of writing. You could become typecast as a particular kind of writer. If you only do sports writing, you could be passed over for an article on another topic because an editor or a client considers you only capable of producing sports copy.

A particular genre often develops its own jargon or terminology, and that could show in your writing. Using sports writing again as an example, what is acceptable reporting there may not go well in a medical article.

Advantages of Generalization

The entire world of freelancing is available to generalists. All the markets are open and just waiting for your prose. As a generalist, you can write about schools today, food tomorrow, and dogs next week. You can write about anything for anybody at anytime.

All markets are your markets. You just need a variety of clips in various fields, and you are a generalist. You can market your general writing services to anyone. You can move between markets as you want. You can approach any possible client or prospect and offer your services as a freelancer.

You do need to be a good researcher and able to write clearly about facts, ideas, and concepts that you might not know much about. For example, if you know nothing about client-server technology deployed by a manufacturer to ensure proper Enterprise Resource Planning, you might have a lot more work to do.

If You Specialize

Develop one or two specialties. Do not make the specialties too tight. It is better to begin with a broader brush, then focus more tightly as you become an expert in your field. For example, you want to write about gardening. There are plenty of markets for this topic: newspapers, some syndicates, and book publishers. You could also find commercial clients and other media that might buy manuscripts. But instead of limiting yourself to just articles about gardening, expand and cover related topics, such as crafts from things garden related or the relationship between gardening and agriculture. You could also cover food preparation (especially food from the garden). As you look for story ideas, you will spot great features. For example, you learn about a farmer that grows a pumpkin patch for inner-city kids so they can enjoy this fall activity. You might find a story about kids growing food that they donate to a local food bank. Or about a new gardening technique that incorporates rare plants into the design.

You will need sources of information, so it will be important to contact potential sources. Contact local universities and find out which ones have horticulture classes. Ask to be added to their media mailing list. Find out from the schools if they have any interesting classes planned or if there are any students that might make a story. Contact government agencies for information, and once again, ask to get on their mailing lists to receive news releases. The Department of Agriculture and Department of Environmental Resources would be especially useful. Identify major businesses that produce products for your specialty. Contact them, and ask them to add your name to their media mailing lists.

Start watching more television shows geared to this topic. Spend a bit more time watching *Do It Yourself Network, Home and Garden*, and shows on PBS. Watch the newspapers for potential leads.

Suddenly, there are many topics available for your stories, articles, and features. And all this happened because you decided to choose a specialty: writing about gardening. Just remember not to specialize so tightly that you cannot see other potential markets that are close to your main interest.

As a generalist, you can quickly turn to new, lucrative markets as they become apparent. Several years ago, environmental writing was in demand. As a generalist, you could quickly seek work on those topics.

Marketing Concerns

Before you make decisions about being a generalist or a specialist, you must consider the markets for your subject areas. As a generalist, all markets are open to you. As a specialist, what is the market situation?

Some areas are wide open, and there is a continuous demand for more material from freelancers. These areas include sports writing, health, and entertainment. If you are freelancing in other than writing services, the same concept applies.

Some areas of specialization are quite competitive, such as travel writing or how-to pieces. Before making a final decision about a specialty, study the markets. How many markets are there for your specialty? If you are a health writer, how big is your marketplace? It is certainly much larger than if you decided to write only articles about boxer dogs.

Making Your Decision

Defining your niche takes time. You might make several false starts before you identify areas that interest you and have a large market potential. But you must start by targeting the markets where you feel you can repeatedly produce good work.

Selling to Publications

As a freelancer, you can almost always find something to prepare and sell to a publication. The list of markets for freelancers is long and varied. Some publications are more open to freelancers than others. Some publishers never use freelancers, while others regularly depend on freelancers to fill their pages.

Tricks of the Trade

There are several tricks that you can use to get a yes from an editor to proceed with your magazine article. They are particularly useful to writers just starting out.

1. *Agree to work on speculation*. You will break into a market much quicker and more readily if you agree to spec work. Most writers want kill fees. Editors will pay them, but do not want to because they may be buying something that

they cannot or will not use. Eliminating that fear makes it much easier for an editor to say yes.

2. *Write smaller pieces.* Realizing they are paid by the word, some writers prefer to write a 3,000-word article, looking forward to cashing the $3,000 paycheck if the rate is $1 a word. It is often easier to write three 1,000-word articles than it is to write one 3,000-word piece. Moreover, the pay is the same! Most writers pitch the longer pieces, trying to get the bigger check. Magazines tend to need the shorter pieces.

3. *Suggest pieces for magazine departments.* Almost all magazines have regular departments each month. Few writers pitch ideas for these departments, but it's a fast way to break into a magazine. The competition is less, the articles are shorter, and the rate is the same. You also prove that you know the magazine when you suggest a piece could fit into a specific department.

Futures Files Guarantees Freelance Success

One of the most important tools you can have at your fingertips in your office is your futures files. This is often what everyone else would take one look at and consider clutter. To a working freelancer, it is future projects.

Your futures files should be divided into at least 12 sections, but you can have additional files if you find it necessary. Each one of these file folders is labeled: January, February, March, etc. You might want to have additional files, one labeled "Book" or another called "URGENT."

Bright Idea
Your futures files can be the source of your future paychecks.

Your futures files system should be simple, but highly organized, and you should have quick and easy access. Those green hanging file folders work best for futures files. You are not limited by size, and stuff just seem to remain neater in them. If you do not have a file cabinet, a cardboard box and regular file folders will work.

On the beginning of each month, you look in the current month's file folder and review its contents. The first of each month will now be a bit busier for you for as long as you remain a working freelancer.

What do you put into the futures files you just created? In a word, everything! This is where you might scribble a note about an idea, and place it in a folder. For example, you think about a great idea for a piece of water gardening. But it's January! Too late for this year. So you file it away in July. You are reading the newspaper, and you see a local company selling an interesting product for gardeners. You rip out its advertisement and place it in your futures files. You find a web site with a news story about something that interests you. You clip a newspaper article with a story about a senior citizen that has been gardening for 50 years.

The idea is that you are clipping, saving, and filing away story ideas for future use. Some things you will want to work on right away. These go into your urgent file. The other items are placed into the proper month.

You are likely to have rollover items. For example, it is June 1 and you are swamped with work! No time to do anything except to finish those projects you have now. So even though you are busy, on June 1 you take the time to put everything in your June folder into your July folder. You will review all the ideas next month.

You are constantly placing items of interest to your specialty into your futures files. Be creative. It could be a handout from a business, a flier, an advertisement, or a magazine.

It should become a habit because it's a necessity for your future income. Don't overlook the value of building your futures files, no matter what type of freelancing you do.

Conversation with Lisa Holton

After a 16-year career in newspapers and magazines, including two years as business editor of the *Chicago Sun-Times*, Lisa Holton decided to open The Lisa Company in 1998. Her company provides writing, editorial, and research services. Holton has taken the extra step of getting her company certified as a women's business enterprise.

These days, she specializes in corporate freelancing and ghostwriting. Her writing business has evolved from traditional journalism. While she wrote query letters and sought editorial assignments at the start, that's not how she finds her work today. "I spend time networking and meeting people," Lisa says. "I attend business events, go to chamber of commerce meetings, and I look for work on the internet."

Initially, The Lisa Company specialized in freelance business journalism. In 1999, Lisa published her first book, *How to be a Value Investor* for McGraw-Hill. *Value Investor* attracted authors looking for an experienced book editor. Lisa's work at *American Demographics* brought her to the attention of several college clients, and the corporate and nonprofit side of the business began to grow. Using her successes, Lisa has been able to grow her freelancing enterprise.

"I'm always thinking about places that would be interesting to work for or where I can make a contribution. If there's a publication or corporate client I want to work for, I always try to introduce myself in writing, usually by e-mail, to its head of communications or another senior official who makes those decisions, just to let them know I'm out there," Lisa says of her ever-ongoing marketing work. "If they respond in a favorable way, I put them on my calendar to re-contact them when they tell me to or at a date four to five months from now."

Lisa follows the rule that marketing never stops. It's what keeps her in business. She says, "But before you contact anyone, you really need to study the organization and get your hands on copies of any projects you think you could make a contribution to. Editors, companies, or organizations don't hire people who don't understand them."

Some of Lisa's marketing is like planting seeds. She waits patiently until the plant grows, and then picks up assignments. "I may not get immediate work, but I'd say I get work later in at least 60 percent of the cases, and some of the folks I contact refer me to other clients who need me," she says. "Business development is a constant activity."

Lisa is fussy about her clients and assignments. It's a lesson that she had to learn. "I think many new freelancers—myself included—fall into the "I'll do anything for money!" trap in their early days of business where they take on any piece of writing work that comes their way, no matter whether it's work they enjoy doing or not," Lisa explains. "Remember, the reason you started your business is so you could do exactly what you want, and loading yourself up just to get cash flow is not only exhausting, but it starts feeling like a real job after awhile. "Always keep in mind that you need to focus on pitching the kinds of work you really enjoy doing," Lisa advises.

"I've maintained a web site since the start of my business, with an outside designer in the driver's seat," Lisa says of www.thelisacompany.com. But keeping a web site updated constantly is critical, and she's in the process of having her site redesigned with a content management system she'll be able to direct. "It's particularly important for writers to have a well-written site with the latest content they've produced," Lisa points out.

11

Expanding Your
Freelance Writing
Business

As a freelancer, you can provide other services to your clients. Some of these services are fun as well as profitable. For example, you might consider offering training. Your client may need help creating letter templates. You could offer to instruct the client's employees on how to create templates or form letters so they are clear and succinct. Your fees

> **Bright Idea**
>
> Often specialized information works best. One freelancer started a small publication about woodworking, only because he could not find the information he needed for his own hobby use. It was the catalyst for a full-fledged publishing business.

could range between $200 to $400 per employee per eight hours of instruction. If your client has 20 employees, the income from this extra service could be substantial.

For many freelancers, the extra services (and sometimes products) do not happen instantly, but rather over time. As you are working as a freelancer and interacting with clients, it may suddenly occur to you that a specific need exists in the marketplace.

One Tallahassee freelancer learned that others needed a voiceover service for photograph slide shows for real estate agents who wanted to showcase the homes they list. He offered this service to a network of photographers, and soon others used his voiceover service. This is the kind of thing that happens often in freelancing. A need is discovered, almost accidentally, and suddenly others purchase that product or service from the freelancer.

Profitable Sidelines

There are profitable sidelines to your freelance writing business. You must first decide what those services might be, and then market them to current clients and future prospects. Some of the related services may have little interest to you, while others might be exactly what you enjoy doing. By adding additional services, new business opportunities (and income) are available to you.

For example, you might start publishing a newsletter. You might launch the newsletter solely as a promotional piece to market your freelance business. It grows in size and scope. It transforms itself from a typical newsletter to a magazine. Over the months of publication, you have people ask about subscribing to your changing publication. Soon you set a subscription fee. As your subscriber base grows, each month your income increases from the paid subscriptions. Many publications have started this humbly. They began as small, kitchen-table created publications, but contained specialized information that a specific segment of the marketplace wanted.

Determining what additional service or product you might want to offer could take some

> **Bright Idea**
>
> Develop services that are in demand. Sure, you could shoe horses and make some money, but the demand is not likely to be that high in today's world. Find those services that clients and prospects want and need now.

time. The list of 25 possible business activities below suggest easy-to-start opportunities that might work for you. Some are simple, additional services. Others require you to create products. All can fit nicely with your regular freelancing. You do not need to consider all of them. Just consider those that interest you and appeal to you. The reasons to add these extras include:

- Additional income from the sales of extra products or services
- Creation of samples to show current and prospective clients
- Improvement of cash flow to cover slow periods

Smart Tip

Tip...

In the real world, simply calling yourself something other than freelancer can open doors that would otherwise be closed. For example, a copywriter is primarily someone who writes for business or advertising. Some potential clients will say they have no need for a freelancer, but embrace your service as a copywriter.

You can often prosper by providing specialized or unique freelance services. One Georgia freelancer didn't find real success until he decided to produce newsletters.

Located near Atlanta, he was not thriving by offering his writing services as a generalist. Then on a whim, he started writing and producing newsletters. He created a newsletter about newsletters, which he used as a marketing piece for his own service as well as a sample to show prospects. He found clients at local business mixers and from chambers of commerce. With all his efforts focused on newsletters, he became a one-stop shop for newsletter production. Within a year, this freelancer had hired two full-time employees. He never opted to require subscriptions for his newsletter.

Here are 25 ideas for expanding your business into other profitable areas:

1. *Teach*. You can teach all kinds of writing to all kinds of people. Don't overlook the opportunities to teach at recreational centers, libraries, schools, community colleges, and even stores. Many organizations that think it is tacky to charge for a seminar or course can change their minds quickly if they are receiving a cut of the tuition. Once you develop a course, you can take it to various outlets.

2. *Information entrepreneur*. This is an idea that can be taken in many different directions. You can write short reports and offer them for sale for a few dollars. It is easier than you may think. Create a document filled with tips. Use a number in the title. For example, a good title might be "56 Ways a Business Can Generate Publicity." Don't pay for advertising. Rather, write a press release announcing its availability and price, and include some excerpts. Send the news release to the editors of magazines and newsletters reaching the booklet's target market. Using today's computer software and the services of a local quick copying center, you can produce the document for a few cents. Set your price

low, perhaps only $2, $3, or $4. Ask that a self-addressed, stamped envelope be included. Now all you have to do is place the documents in the envelope as the orders pour in. One entrepreneurial writer did just what is described here, and sold 3,000 booklets in one month at $3 each, for a gross income of $9,000. She only printed the quantity she needed as orders came in, and kept the duplication cost at 18 cents each. She made roughly $8,460 from one idea.

3. *Sell informational reports.* Taking the last idea a bit further, you can also sell informational reports, but at higher prices. The informational reports can be sold for a few dollars, or they can be sold for more. Look for trends and new needs for information. Whether in print or digital form, practical information that solves an immediate problem can sell at prices far out of proportion to its size. One writer sells reports, starting at $4.95 and up through his fax-on-demand system and his web site, as well as by sending printed material through the mail. An example of the kind of information that might sell well is a listing of the 100 best sources of products that can be sold on eBay. Everyone actively trying to sell more is a potential customer. You can license your reports to others to sell, too.

4. *Photography.* Many publications, particularly smaller ones, prefer to purchase photos with manuscripts. Often the amount you are paid for photos can be more than you are paid for the writing. Selling the photos or artwork makes sense. You do not need an extremely expensive camera system. Just a decent 35 mm with good lenses is what it takes. Learn how to frame your subjects; there are often inexpensive photography classes available in the community. Sometimes you can sell the photography, and not the manuscript.

5. *Consulting.* Nonfiction writers that develop a specialty can often land lucrative consulting fees. This happens often to technical writers, especially those working the information systems areas. Others that easily land consulting contracts are those that specialize in sales and marketing, business, and finance. One writer that specializes in writing about trash removal often consults for businesses in finding ways to reduce the costs of waste management. Consulting fees can start at $30 an hour and go to $10,000 a day, depending on the skills and demands of the consultant.

6. *Presentations creator.* Everyone is so busy today that they often don't even have the time to create their own presentations for sales meetings, conventions, or training seminars. This business can easily supplement your freelance income. Contact printers and quick copy shops, and let them know you are available. You can also develop contacts at the local chamber of commerce.

7. *Ghostwriter.* As a ghostwriter, you get no byline, no credit. You just do the work. All you get is the money. One financial services writer got $60,000 for all rights to the work. It took him four months of writing and editing part time

to earn that paycheck. Ghost writing assignments are sometimes hard to locate, but if you look for them, they can be found. You can also let publishers and agents know that you are available for ghost writing assignments.

8. *Resume service.* Just like tax preparers, people would rather go to a professional than do the work themselves. Even though there is a plethora of resume creation software available, you can make big dollars fast and steadily by providing resume writing services. A small classified ad in the Sunday newspaper is all it takes to get started.

9. *Newspaper correspondent or stringer.* Working for a local newspaper is not going to make you rich, but it is going to help you make great contacts, get ideas for stories that could go into national publications, and help buy groceries. Most newspapers hire some writers as newspaper correspondents or stringers to cover local news (school board meetings, town council meetings, etc.). You can often break in with just one clip and a willingness to work evenings or on weekends.

10. *Syndication.* At one time, syndication was a great source of income for writers, but these markets are drying up and tough to break into. That does not mean you should not try. You can go to an established syndicate, or you can self-syndicate your column or articles. One writer has built an empire by self-publishing a column about home improvement and making your home more energy efficient. He also sells his readers reports via the internet and his web site, as well as through the mail. His operation is so large now that he turns down offers to be syndicated by the big syndicates. He knows he is making more money doing it on his own rather than working for others. Check out this operation at www.dulley.com.

11. *Self-publish.* You have to be careful when you think about self-publishing your writing. Your work has to be 100 percent professional, top quality, and shining. And you have to be willing to run a publishing company. If you are, consider self-publishing as a great income stream. Go slow, learn everything you can, and start small with little publications or books. Many large publishers started on the kitchen table, and you can, too, if you have the drive. To succeed, you must have a clearly defined specialty. Make sure you can find an easily defined audience for the items you want to publish.

12. *Web site informational sales.* You can start a web site that charges for access to its information. The information can be anything that is not readily available elsewhere free. Selling information can be highly lucrative. Check out www.lesko.com. Matthew Lesko is that animated character that wears wild suits and seems to be running on high octane. He sells all kinds of information about our government and various programs. He tells people how to find grant money, loans, and government giveaways. Selling information can make

you a fortune. Look at what www.wooden-horsepub.com is doing. There are thousands of examples available on the internet. Starting on the internet can keep your start-up costs down.

13. *Editing services.* You can offer editorial services to other writers and publishers. Freelance editing can be profitable, fun, and provide fill-in work. Some freelance editors get so busy they have to turn down work. Check out the classified advertisements in a current *Writer's Digest* and one from five years ago. The same ads are running. These editors stay in business by providing fast, dependable, and honest service. And it is lucrative. The average going rate is $2 a double-spaced page. One writer turned editor had to stop because he was too successful as an editor and had no time to write. He wanted to write, so he gave up the editing business. For five years after he stopped advertising, he was still receiving requests for his editing services.

14. *Public relations.* There is always a need for public relations (PR) writing. Local organizations (nonprofits) and businesses can keep you quite busy. Preparing press kits, press releases, managing events, and even writing articles for publication are some of the things busy PR writers do. Many freelance writers break into this and eventually leave the freelance writing world in favor of the PR world.

15. *Desktop publishing.* You can still supplement your writing income by providing desktop publishing services. You should go after more difficult jobs, such as books, manuals, and technical training guides. Offering editing and writing services makes you stand out from others with word processing software and a laser printer.

16. *Newsletter publisher.* As publisher of your own newsletter, you control the entire content. The more specialized the newsletter, the more in demand it could become. You make your money through subscriptions, by selling advertising, or some combination of both. Some newsletters become so profitable for their publishers that they are able to build huge publishing companies or they sell them to another publisher after they have been developed and are profitable. Newsletter publishing has built such publications as *Entrepreneur* magazine and the *Lundberg Report*. There are many books on the subject, and even a small newsletter can make a substantial income for its publisher.

17. *Copywriter.* Advertising agencies constantly require a stable of freelance copywriters. A resume and a sample or two is what it takes to get your first assignment. The trick is to get a face-to-face meeting with someone in the agency. If you do good work, your phone will be ringing.

18. *Radio spots writer.* If you can write 30-, 45-, or 60-second spots with a bit of a flair and humor, you will be in demand once the radio stations know about you. You need some samples, a creative mind, and the determination to meet with the sales manager of every nearby radio station. One writer got turned down

flat, until he asked if he could also sell the advertising for the commercial. The sales manager then agreed, knowing there was nothing to lose. The writer contacted an advertiser on a competing station, and wrote three different spots. The advertiser loved the new copy, thought it was much more creative. He agreed to buy the ads on the new station, as long as he could use the ads on the current station he was using. The writer was paid a commission for the advertising, a writing fee, and he was smart enough to follow up with his new client. He got the client to write a letter to the sales manager, praising the new ad campaign, which really did work. The sales manager was smart enough to recognize a good thing, and the writer was placed under contract to write ad spots.

19. *Technical writing*. If you can write in clean and easy-to-understand language, often step-by-step directions, you can become a technical writer. Used in many industries, a technical writer produces documentation and other manuscripts for new products, procedures, or applications. The pay is usually high, often starting around $30 an hour for beginners. Some jobs require on-site work, while others allow you to do all the work at home. Many of these assignments are found for you by employment agencies or headhunters. All you need is an updated resume and a writing sample.

20. *Web content provider*. Businesses and organizations dedicated to having an active web site soon learn they need new and fresh content to keep visitors returning. You can be a web content provider. Generic information can be sold and resold to different, noncompeting sites. For example, you can sell content on how to get a merchant account (a special bank account for businesses that allows the acceptance of credit cards) at the best possible terms. That article could be sold to web sites designed for dentists, car mechanics, small businesses, antique dealers, and so on. It just takes some imagination and the willingness to put a program together.

21. *Community cookbook*. If you have a knack for cooking, consider putting together a community cookbook. Contact a local organization to get its name on the book. Set your fee. Solicit recipes from the community, and get the cookbook printed. The organization sells the books, and keeps the profits. Plenty of free publicity for everyone. The more work you do, the larger your fee.

22. *Specialized local publishing*. There are many possibilities as a local or regional publisher. One writer publishes *Senior News*, a throwaway newspaper that is now filled with advertisements of interest to the over-50 population. Articles on local seniors, along with a mix of pieces on subjects of interest to this segment of the population fill the always-growing publication. It has grown so fast that it now sponsors a spring and fall senior expo. Another writer started a similar publication for parents with preschool kids. The advertising pays the way with these types of publications.

23. *Local history guides*. These guides are another form of self-publishing. You prepare local historical guides: booklets, pamphlets, or even small books. You then sell them wholesale to the local gift shops tourists visit. Some popular titles that always work are ghost stories of locally haunted sites. One writer created five of these guides, sells thousands of them each year, and provides guided tours to the haunted sites.

24. *How-to publisher*. If you have a writing specialty, it gets easy to publish how-to guides. These guides can be booklets or reports on CD-ROMs or in book format. People spend money on how-to information. How to buy a house with no money down, how to make money on eBay, and how to build birdhouses for fun and profit are some topics that could easily be expanded and sold. How-to publishers grow rapidly, and soon income can be substantial.

25. *Corporate writer*. Writing for corporate America can be quite lucrative. One writer earned $35,000 for writing a book about a large corporation's founder to celebrate the company's fiftieth anniversary. Another writer was kept busy writing training courses and handout materials for a corporate training center.

Adding Additional Services to Your Clients

Don't overlook opportunities for offering additional services to your current clients. Keep in touch with your clients and offer to provide services they are not currently buying from you. For example, if your clients are publishers, offer to do copyediting. If your clients are local businesses, offer to develop letter templates. If you are working for the advertising department as a product copywriter, ask about expanding into the public relations department. You can provide research assistance, proofreading, or any other related service.

Tip...

Smart Tip

It is often easier to get more work for a current client than it is to get work from a new prospect. While you should always be looking for new clients, be sure your current clients know you are available for additional work assignments.

Special Skills or Equipment Required

As you consider these ideas, you can see that some of the suggestions require special skills or additional equipment. If you were to choose to offer photography services, you might not only need to learn photography skills but also purchase thousands of dollars worth of equipment. That will only make sense to you if it is something you really want to do and if it makes sense from a business standpoint to do so.

Some of the skills you need you may have to learn, through self-study or taking courses. Many community colleges or vocational schools offer evening or weekend classes that can help you develop a skill you can use in your freelancing business.

12

Copyediting and Proofreading Services

One fast and easy way to expand your freelance business is to offer copyediting and/or proofreading services. You'll be amazed at how many potential clients will say, "No, we don't need/want/use freelancers." But if you offer copyediting or proofreading, the door suddenly opens.

Copyediting

Copy refers to written material to be typeset for printing. Copyediting is the process by which an editor makes formatting changes and grammatical improvements to this written material. One who performs the task of copyediting is usually called a copyeditor. In many cases, a copyeditor will be the only person other than the writer of the material to read the entire text before its publication.

The copyeditor's job is to make the copy clear, correct, concise, comprehensible, and consistent. (often referred to as the five Cs). Copyediting typically includes correcting spelling, punctuation, and grammatical errors. Copyeditors also make sure the final text follows a specific style. For example, if the word "web site" is used rather than "website." Copyeditors also add standardized format elements, such as headers, footers, and headlines. These elements of the final publication design must be determined before the typesetter or desktop publisher can prepare a final copy for proofing.

The copyeditor is expected see that the text flows well, and makes logical sense. He looks for missing facts or confused wording. He also reviews the text to make sure it will cause no legal problems for the publisher. A copyeditor may abridge text, commonly referred to as "cutting" or "trimming." He may also add or write short pieces of text to insert into the copy.

Who Needs Copyeditors?

The list of potential clients that need copyeditors is long. Obviously, any publisher of newspapers, magazines, or books requires copyeditors. No matter what the size of the publisher, copyediting opportunities are usually available. Some other local organizations that are likely to need freelancers that offer copyediting service include:

- Accountants and accounting firms
- Advertising agencies

Beware!
Some potential clients who regularly use copyeditors will ask you to take a test. Don't be surprised if you are asked to take one, and don't worry about it—if your grammar is good.

- Chambers of commerce
- College/university students, especially those for whom English is a second language and those who need to complete a thesis or dissertation for graduation
- Corporations
- Government agencies
- Individual authors
- Law firms
- Not-for-profit organizations
- Professional associations
- Public relations firms
- Schools, colleges, and universities
- Small local businesses

> **Tip...**
>
> **Smart Tip**
>
> Many companies on the internet offer copyediting services. Many are constantly looking for copyeditors. Locate these companies by searching for "copyediting" on your favorite search engine.

To learn more about copyediting, check out the American Copy Editors Society at www.copydesk.org/.

Finding Clients

Locating clients is not that difficult for freelancers copyeditors. Many can be found locally. However, with the internet, clients can be served from anywhere.

Using lists of local organizations or businesses, contact the communications director or department of each. A simple business letter describing your service is all it takes to generate business. Some copyeditors also prepare a simple brochure for potential clients. Networking among local businesspeople can often generate work for a freelance copyeditor. Larger organizations tend to be more likely to hire freelancers.

Another source of income is internet companies that offer copyediting services. These companies, easily located by using a search engine, often need copyeditors. Pay varies, and rates may not be as high as for local work. Nevertheless, these companies can provide you with work during slack periods.

For clients with continuous copyediting needs, breaking in is frequently a two-step process. Often, a smaller job is given as a test to a new copyeditor. The finished work is then analyzed. If the work is good, larger projects are assigned.

Special Skills

Copyeditors need a good grasp of grammar, and the ability to make written copy clear and concise. Copyeditors help writers say what it is they are trying to say by making their prose easier to read and understand. To do this in a way compositors and printers (often overseas now) can follow, copyeditors must know and use standard proofreaders' marks. The Copyeditors' Marks example below depicts the most commonly used proofreaders' marks.

Copyeditors' Marks

Symbol	Meaning	Example
♻ or ✄ or ᧒	delete	take it out
◠	close up	print as o ne word
♻	delete and close up	close up
∧ or ⟩ or ⌃	caret	insert here ⟨ something
#	insert a space	put onehere
eq#	space evenly	space evenly ∧ where∧indicated
stet	let stand	let marked text stand as set
tr	transpose	change order the
/	used to separate two or more marks and often as a concluding stroke at the end of an insertion	
⊏	set farther to the left	⌐ too far to the right
⊐	set farther to the right	too⌐ far to the left
⌒	set as ligature (such as æ)	encyclopaedia
⹀	align horizontally	alignment
‖	align vertically	‖ align with surrounding text
✗	broken character	imperfect
◻	indent or insert em quad space	
¶	begin a new paragraph	

Copyeditors' Marks, continued

Symbol	Meaning	Example
SP	spell out	set 5 lbs. as five pounds
cap	set in CAPITALS	set nato as NATO
sm cap or s.c.	set in SMALL CAPITALS	set signal as SIGNAL
lc	set in lowercase	set South as south
ital	set in *italic*	set oeuvre as *oeuvre*
rom	set in roman	set mensch as mensch
bf	set in **boldface**	set important as **important**
= or -/ or ⌃ or /H/	hyphen	multi-colored
¦/N or en or /N/	en dash	1965–72
¦/M or em or /M/	em (or long) dash	Now—at last!—we know.
∨	superscript or superior	as in πr^2
∧	subscript or inferior	as in H_2O
⌄ or ⋎	centered	for a centered dot in $p \cdot q$
⸲	comma	
⸲	apostrophe	
⊙	period	
; or ;/	semicolon	
: or ⊙	colon	
❝❞ or ⸶⸷	quotation marks	
(/)	parentheses	
[/]	brackets	
OK/?	query to author: has this been set as intended?	

What to Charge

Copyeditors often are compensated by the hour or by the page. Pay varies depending on location, your ability to negotiate rates, and even how much work is involved. For example, a professional writer may need little work to her manuscript, but a student who does not speak or write English very well may need extensive work. Charging $3 per page may make sense in the first instance, but could be quite unprofitable in the second.

Pay ranges from a low of $1 per page to a high of $10 per page. The lower pay range is for manuscripts that need little work. The higher pay range is for manuscripts that need extensive editing, almost a rewrite. Rates can be higher for technical topics, such as scientific or medical topic documents. They can also be higher if your skills include translation of another language. Copyeditors often establish a minimum charge. For small jobs, the minimum is $15 to $25.

Proofreading

Proofreading is similar to but distinctively different from copyediting. The proofreader reviews the proof (typeset copy) from the printer. The material has been edited and typeset. A proofreader looks for mistakes in the final production, catching them before printing, publication, and distribution. She is the final line of defense before printing. Obvious—and not so obvious errors— are detected and corrected before a costly printing run is made.

> **Tip...**
>
> **Smart Tip**
> Copyeditors work with manuscripts. Proofreaders work with typeset manuscripts, or in other words, text that needs proofed before it is sent to a printing press.

The proofreader checks everything possible, from spelling in the headlines to page numbering. He makes sure photos match captions, and captions match illustrations. He checks to make sure everything is "correct." In many cases, the proofreader is last person that sees the text before the printer is authorized to start the press and finish the production of the material.

Proofreaders have developed marks that are used by them and the printer to correct errors in the typesetting. For example, if a letter in a word needs to be capitalized, that is, go from lowercase to uppercase, the proofreader underlines the letter three times, writes "cap" in the margin, and circles the word "cap." Proofreaders use red pencils to mark their changes to typeset material. Proofreaders marks are the same as those used in the copyediting examples listed on pages 106 and 107.

Who Needs Proofreading Services?

Just as in copyediting, the list of potential clients that need proofreading services is long. Obviously, any publisher utilizes proofreaders. Depending on the size of the publisher, proofreaders may be regular employees. Others use freelancers to take on their proofreading needs, making opportunities available for you.

A good source of referral business is your local printers. By contacting printers, you can often find work. Printers need their customers to get their proofreading done quickly so they can finish the printing job. Many printers maintain lists of freelance proofreaders to give to their customers who need this service and some hire freelancer's directly. Companies that need freelance copyeditors tend to need proofreaders. See the list on pages 104 and 105.

Finding Clients

You can use the same methods for locating proofreading clients as you would for copyediting clients, but clients are more numerous. Many smaller businesses would never hire copyeditors but will hire proofreaders. For example, sales organizations (or individual sales representatives) must produce sales proposals. Although there may be only a few copies produced (usually on a computer printer), salespeople often want an "extra set of eyes" to review important proposals. Finding this work requires more networking.

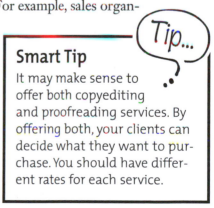

> **Smart Tip**
> It may make sense to offer both copyediting and proofreading services. By offering both, your clients can decide what they want to purchase. You should have different rates for each service.

Finding mistakes is the main objective of proofreading. In most cases, others have reviewed the material several times. As the proofreader, your task is to catch editing mistakes and printing errors. The idea is to distribute only a perfect piece.

What to Charge

Proofreading generally pays less than copyediting because material needing proofing has usually been copyedited. This is not always the case, but it is the general assumption.

It is more difficult to set a per page rate for proofreading. This is because of the various types of typeset materials. Even the number of words per page can vary greatly. Some designs might have about 200 words per book page, while others could have double that number. A brochure might have a lot of copy, or a little.

Because of these variables, proofreading is often charged at an hourly rate, rather than per page. Rates start at a low of $15 per hour, and can be as high as $40 per hour for technical or scientific material. Most freelance proofreaders charge $20 to $25 per hour.

13

Freelancing by the Numbers

There are very few businesses that spirited entrepreneurs can jump into without a large capital investment. Fortunately, freelance writing is one that requires little initial capital. It is likely that you already have much of the equipment and many of the supplies you need. If you already own a personal computer, you can get started with a modest investment.

Don't over purchase in the initial stages of starting your freelancing service. It is often better to operate on a shoestring and with meager equipment than to drain your savings account. While you might want a new computer, hold on to your cash until your business is successfully launched and you have developed a steady stream of clients.

Inventory

As a freelancer, you do not need to purchase or stock any inventory for resale. You need some office supplies, which you may already have. If not, you need to purchase some items to keep on hand as you launch your freelancing service. Some of the miscellaneous supply items you need include:

- Bond paper (case)
- An extra cartridge for the computer's printer
- Envelopes (business number 10)
- Envelopes (9-by-12-inch clasps)
- Pens and pencils
- File folders
- Stapler and staples, tape, paper clips
- Calculator
- CDs or DVDs to deliver to your clients and to make backup copies of projects.

Most of these items are inexpensive. If you don't have any of them, you should be able to get everything you need for $150 to $200.

Bright Idea

Consider joining a warehouse club to save on your office supplies. Sam's Club, Costco, and BJ's Wholesale Club are just some of the places that offer significant savings.

Smart Tip

Tip...

Make sure you have enough money to purchase postage. You will need several rolls of stamps during the start-up period as you market your services.

Start-Up Expenses

The initial start-up expense can be much higher if you are starting with no computer, office equipment, or supplies. If you already own a computer and desk, a printer, and some office supplies, the amount you need to spend is far less. The Start-Up Expenses table on page 113 depicts two hypothetical freelance businesses. One assumes the freelancer already owns

Start-Up Expenses

	Freelancer with most equipment	Freelancer purchasing most equipment
Technology Purchases		
Computer: Desktop		$1,500
Computer: Laptop		$1,500
Monitor		$300
Scanner	$250	$250
External back-up drive	$125	$300
Fax machine	$150	$250
Laser printer: Color		$700
Laser printer: Black		$200
Label printer		$100
Copier		$600
Software		
Microsoft Office	$250	$600
Quick Books	$100	$350
Antivirus software	$50	$50
Office Furniture		
Desk		$700
Chair		$500
File cabinets	$125	$300
Bookcases	$100	$450
Office Supplies		
Business cards	$20	$40
Miscellaneous supplies	$150	$250
Postage meter		$120
Uninterrupted power supply		$125
Total Expenditures	**$1,320**	**$9,185**

most equipment and supplies, while the other assumes that the freelancer decided to go with the top-of-the-line equipment to outfit her office.

As you can see, the range of expenditures on your initial start-up for equipment and supplies varies greatly. It really depends on what you currently own and how much you decide to spend on those items you don't own. You can save on a lot on start-up costs if you hold off purchasing things you don't need initially. As an example, don't invest in a photocopier to start. Use the photocopier at your local library to limit your cash outlay.

Tally It Up

After your initial start-up costs, monthly overhead expenses need to be considered. The good news again is that with a freelance business, your monthly operating costs are small. In the Monthly Overhead Expenses table below, the monthly expenses are represented for both a bare-bones home office and a small office outside the home.

Monthly Overhead Expenses

Monthly Operating Expenses		
	Low	High
Rent	0	$500
Phone	$50	$150
Utilities	$0	$50
Postage	$50	$150
Internet service	$40	$65
Web hosting	$5	$25
Miscellaneous expenses	$25	$100
Total Expenses	**$170**	**$1,040**

Monthly Net Income

Projected monthly income: $_____

Projected monthly expenses: $_____

Subtract monthly expenses from monthly income: $_____

which equals your projected montly net income $_____

Project insurance costs: $_____

Projected taxes: $_____

Subtract projected insurance costs and
projected taxes from projected monthly net income $_____

which is your monthly net income $_____

The formula for your net income is simple. Your monthly expenses are subtracted from your monthly income. The difference is your pretax income. See Monthly Net Income for an example of this. From that amount, you must pay your taxes and insurances, such as life, hospitalization, and disability coverage.

Smart Tip

Tip...

Always look for ways to save money. If you can save just $100 a month in expenditures, that's $1,200 a year right to your bottom line. You don't have to work harder to make this extra money, just smarter!

Financing the Freelance Business

Initial start-up costs (for those items you don't already own) can be financed with a credit card. Because in most cases freelancers commence their businesses quickly and inexpensively, there is no need to seek a small business loan.

In some instances, grants are available to writers. They usually offer a stipend while writing or researching some worthwhile or scholarly topic. Approval often takes months. Most freelancers do not wait for funds to become available, but rather jump right into the business.

The larger a freelancer's savings account, the better. Having a cash reserve eliminates the need for begging for work or looking desperately for any assignment.

> ### ⚠ Beware!
>
> If you use your personal credit cards in your freelancing business, make sure you are paying the balances off each month. If you are taking cash advances each month to pay bills, you are heading toward a financial disaster.

Keeping money in a savings account for those times when cash flow is slow is always beneficial. There are times in a freelancer's life when no money is coming in one month, and thousands arrive the following month. It is during the low times that savings accounts become crucial and keep the freelancer afloat.

The amount you need to start often depends on your resourcefulness and practicality. It is possible to say you need to buy a new car for your freelancing business. But in reality, the transportation you currently use is likely to be just fine. The desk you have now might be a rescue from a yard sale, but as long as it works, it should be OK for your start-up. Hold on to your cash as much as possible, and work with what you have. Plan to purchase larger items later. Always start out with the bare minimum, and slowly grow from there. Once your business grows and prospers, you can then acquire those extras without having a crushing debt hanging over your head.

Insurance

Depending on your current situation, you may need to purchase different forms of insurance, or you may need none. Always shop for insurance. It may take you two hours, for example, to solicit quotes. That is time well served if you save money. A $100 yearly savings means you made the equivalent of $50 per hour.

Bookkeeping for the Freelancer

It's fairly easy to maintain your bookkeeping. You can do it the high-tech way, with your computer and an accounting program, or the low-tech way, with a simple ledger book. Because this is such a simple business, you log your income and your expenses. You are not likely to have many income entries (because you can only do so many projects). You list your expenses (and again, you are not likely to have many, but you will have some, such as internet service, web hosting, phone, etc.).

Keep your receipts, and keep them on file for your accountant or professional tax preparer. Consult with your tax experts about what is and is not deductible. Claim every legitimate deduction you are entitled to and that you can verify with your recordkeeping.

Invoicing Clients

Many clients need an invoice before processing your check. If you are using a computerized bookkeeping system, the software will generate an invoice for you. If you need to generate an invoice outside of accounting software, use your word processor to create a simple and professional invoice similar to the Sample Invoice below.

Sample Invoice

George Sheldon
Post Office Box 6238
Lancaster, PA 17607

September 7, 20xx   Terms: Net 10

Sold to:

Susan Smith

Sunnyside Publishing

5545 Main Street

Sunnyside, PA 19199

Ghost writing—*How to Start a Car Repair Business* $5,500

Total due: $5,500

THANK YOU!

14

Honing Your Work Habits

In this final chapter, you learn how to develop and fine tune your work habits, which will increase your production and your income. To do so, you must understand the freelancer's place in the publishing world. Consider how nonfiction freelance writers fit in the news system, what they can expect from magazines, and how they can market their skills.

The News Market

There are three main areas of news. First, there is hard news. In today's world, this news is disseminated to the masses via broadcast media (radio and television), newspapers, and the internet. Second, there is background news, which is less immediate, but still current. It is offered via magazines and increasingly, the internet. Lastly, there are books. For nonfiction writers, books are the last place where news is assembled and information is disseminated.

Suppose, for example, there is an airplane crash and a well-liked celebrity is killed. In the news cycle, all television and radio news broadcasts contain the story. The internet news sites include articles about the celebrity. The following week, the news magazines publish articles about the crash, and the celebrity. Web sites continue to post information about the crash and the celebrity. Regular magazines publish cover stories about the celebrity, but because of the cycle time, they are not on the newsstand until two to three months later. Finally, several books are written and published about the life and times of the celebrity. They are finally available in about a year. Information remains available on the internet about the celebrity. Such is the news cycles in today's world of publishing.

The way a news story breaks determines the opportunities that exist for freelance writers. Consider the time line in the Sample News Cycle below.

Sample News Cycle

Today/Tomorrow	Next Week	1 to 3 Months	More than 3 Months
Broadcast news: TV, radio, internet, newspapers	News magazines, internet	Magazines, internet	Some magazines, books
Freelance opportunities are low	Freelance opportunities are low to medium	Freelance opportunities are high	Freelance opportunities are high

From this chart, you can see that the further away you are from the actual news event, the greater your opportunities are to sell your services as a nonfiction writer. Staff writers are used more by the news organizations for breaking news. Staff writers are not used as much for stories and articles far from the date of an event. And book publishers seldom hire staff writers to produce their books.

Magazines

There are many different markets available for the freelance nonfiction writer. Most writers think of markets on a narrow basis, but there are many markets available to you, if you seek them out. Have you considered greeting card companies? Still a staple of the freelance nonfiction writer is the magazine market. Many of the things that you learn about marketing and selling to magazines can be used in all the other markets. For that reason, I am going to look closely at this market segment.

Writing for Magazines

There are over 15,000 consumer magazines published each month, so there is a constant need for nonfiction writers and their work.

All magazines need good writing. They want fresh ideas. They are looking for freelance nonfiction writers right now. Why else would publishers spend money on staff to cull through stacks of unsolicited manuscripts and query letters, looking for potential article ideas? Without fresh ideas from fresh talent, their publications would wither and die like last year's gourds on a vine.

> **Tip...**
>
> **Smart Tip**
> There are more than 10,000 trade magazines in North America, and probably more than 18,000 internationally. Nonfiction writers often overlook this huge market.

In an old movie, Mel Gibson received such an electrical shock in the bathtub that he was suddenly able to know what women want. You will wish it were that easy with an editor. It would be so nice to just be jolted once while soaking in your bath and have that power. What do editors want? They do not know what they want. They only know they want good writing and fresh ideas that fit their publication. They do not know what they really want until they see it. That is where you, the nonfiction writer, appear.

Magazine Musts

Most magazines have a standard type of article that they want and consistently use. Magazines publish particular article types over and over, month in, month out, year in, year out. The most popular article types are:

- *Exposé.* This article exposes or reports on an injustice. Stories on someone wrongly convicted of murder, a corrupt government official, or passing kids that failed classes are in this category.

- *How-to.* These articles are the mainstay of many publications. Most special interest magazines are by their nature how-to magazines: How to write and be published, repair a car, plant a garden, hunt for a bear, raise a puppy, catch a fish, or crochet a doily. Within that context, how-to articles focus on specific issues and problems. They teach the reader how to do something new or unusual, solve a common problem, develop a skill, or increase personal enjoyment.

Bright Idea

You do not have to be a doctor or a specialist to write on health and safety. You can quote sources in your article, giving your piece authority. Many markets prefer such articles from the perspective of a typical participant and do not want articles written because they are in a scholarly, hard-to-comprehend style.

- *Product reviews.* These articles review a product or products for the reader. The piece compares features and prices. An example is an article about accounting software for small business owners.

- *Service reviews.* Much like a product review, these articles review specific services. An example is an article about package shipment services for sellers of products on eBay.

- *Make-overs.* These articles focus on a before and after scenario. The idea is to show how to make improvements. Used by women's magazines to show how to improve makeup and hairstyles, this format can be used in any number of situations. For example, a typical article is how to organize a child's playroom.

- *Health and safety.* Many special interest areas involve health and/or safety issues, such as how to handle common emergencies, how to avoid safety hazards, or how to maintain or improve your health by participating in a specific activity. These articles are used more than ever in sports and recreation magazines. Nutrition articles also fall in this category.

- *Current news.* All magazines want articles in their subject areas that are news based. For example, health care providers would need to read an article about a change in a law that requires them to report certain findings to a government regulatory agency.

- *Seasonal.* Some activities are seasonal. For example, an article on how to capture colorful fall leaves on film could quickly be accepted by a magazine that attracts a mature or retirement-age reader.

- *Destination*. Travel pieces are used by many publications. Almost any will use a destination piece, as long as it is customized to their readership. For example, a parenting magazine might like a piece on child-oriented museums. Be sure that whatever is happening at your "destination" appeals to the magazine's readers.

> **Tip...**
>
> ### Smart Tip
> Many new writers try to sell personal experiences written in a first-person format. They seldom sell. Does anyone really want to read 1,000 words about your experiences getting your first kitten? Magazines that use these types of articles are often flooded with amateurish pieces.

- *Historical background*. Some magazines seek historical background information pieces. An example might be the history of the Chevrolet Bel Air for an automotive publication.

- *Profiles*. Profile articles usually highlight someone whose work has achieved recognition, who has made a significant contribution to the field, or who is doing something unique or unusual. Some magazines use them; others do not. Some also use personal experiences.

So not only should you develop a writing specialty, you should also strive to develop additional outlets for that specialty. For example, once you master the how-to article, you can produce them for many different publications quickly and easily.

Working the Markets

It is now time to begin working your markets. You need a list of 25 to 30 primary markets, based on your specialty. If your specialty is financial writing, for example, your market list would include all the markets most likely to use your articles.

You should divide your markets into three categories: top, standard, and poor. The standard market category is where most of your markets will be listed. These markets offer moderate, but not top, pay. They can consistently provide income and publish your writing. Poor markets are those that you do not want to use, but will sell to as a last resort. For example, you come up with a great idea, and for no explainable reason, it does not sell to any of your top or standard markets. You still think it will sell, so you send it to a market in your poor category.

Top markets are the ones you strive to break into and work regularly. These are the big prestigious magazines that pay $1 a word or more. You want to be trying to break into these bigger, better markets.

Pay on Publication

There are publications that will only pay you when they publish your article. Never work for these markets! Only if the name of this book were *How to Become a Starving Writer* would I think of recommending that you do any work here. These publications can hold your work for years. You may never be paid. Try to take something out of a store and not pay for it. For example, it's December, and they have a great sale on lawn mowers. You will not use it until April, so you promise to come back then and pay for it. You would soon be in jail for shoplifting.

Pay on publication is a scheme in which publishers are stealing from you. They are keeping you from eating or paying your bills. You cannot sell the piece elsewhere while they are holding it, especially if they bought First North American Serial Rights. These are the kind of publications you want your competitors to write for. Let your competitors be tied up and busy with these markets, so you can proceed to market your work to pay-on-acceptance publications. Do not include any pay-on-publication markets on your marketing list.

Number of Queries

One of the questions that new freelancers often ask is, "How many queries should I have in the mail at one time?" The answer is simple: As many as you can.

You should always, no matter how busy you are, be marketing your services and attempting to get a yes from editors. Until your phone is ringing, you should be spending 60 to 80 percent of your writing time sending out queries and seeking work. If you have nothing to do, you should be studying markets, looking for ideas, and submitting more queries.

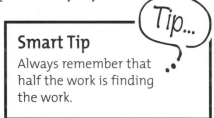

Smart Tip

Always remember that half the work is finding the work.

Even when you are busy with writing assignments, you should be sending queries. At the minimum, you should be spending 20 percent of your time seeking work. If you are working a 40-hour, 5-day week, you should always spend at least one full day marketing. Of course, you can do two half days, or whatever other schedule works for you. But in the beginning, you need to spend much more time marketing.

Because you are specializing, you need to repitch ideas from one publication to the next, if it is turned down. For example, suppose you want to do an article about cars that are painted to advertise a business. You create a simple log like that in the sample on page 125.

In this example, you sent the piece to *Small Business*, but it was rejected. Immediately, you sent it on to *Motor Trend*. If it is not accepted there, the idea will be sent to *New Business Magazine*. You can see that it takes some paperwork to keep track

Sample Query Log

Article Idea	Market	Out	Response
Car Ads	Small Business	1–7	1–29 Reject
	Motor Trend	1–29	
	New Business Magazine		

of your ideas and your submissions. This is not wasted time. The bookkeeping you do on tracking your submissions will result in more sales. You will be able to spot dead queries—ideas that died on the vine but are still viable and should continue to be marketed. If you do not hear positively from a publication in six weeks, assume the idea is not wanted, and move onto the next market.

Working Your Top Markets

Those markets that you identified as your top markets should be contacted every 30 to 60 days. You want to keep a query letter floating in their office regularly. Remember that it will take time to break in. These are top markets, but that does not mean that you should not keep trying. If you are professional in your approach and keep at it, you will get the door to crack open. When it does, be ready to walk through it as a professional.

Consistent Marketing

To be successful as a nonfiction writer, you must consistently market your ideas and make pitches to editors. This has to occur on a regular schedule. Do not shirk this responsibility.

As you develop your query letters, you will be able to use the copy and paste feature of your word processor, making it much easier to produce your queries faster. The information about you and your letter close can be reused. You can even keep your target market information (editor name, publication, address) electronically stored so you can reuse it repeatedly.

To avoid marketing is to give yourself a prescription for not publishing. You must constantly and consistently keep trying. Remember, too, that you will receive rejection letters. It is part of the business.

Consistent Writing

Just as you must constantly market, you must also constantly and consistently write. Each day, at the same time, you should take your position in front of your computer and write. If it is writing query letters, that is certainly OK. But keep writing! Do not slack off.

Avoid Time Wasters

You must have your work time, and you must produce work. If you are not producing, something is wrong. It could be that you are wasting too much time. Avoid computer games, e-mail lists, and discussion boards that tend to waste time or divert you. It is easy to get absorbed and waste time on the internet.

Take necessary breaks, but maintain your work schedule. Make sure you are not disturbed for long periods by your pets, children, or spouse. Watch out for long, non-productive telephone conversations.

If you have to rearrange your schedule because of an external reason, such as going to the dentist, it is OK. However, if you lost two hours of production time due to that appointment, try to make it up.

Appendix A
Formatting a Manuscript

The following pages show the proper way to format a manuscript.

George Sheldon

Post Office Box 6238

Lancaster, PA 17607-6238

Phone: (717) 555-5555

Fax: (717) 555-5555

E-mail: gs@georgegsheldon.com

Federal ID # 21-00000000

First North American Serial Rights

Approximate Word Count—900

©2011 George Sheldon

HOW TO FORMAT A MANUSCRIPT

By George G. Sheldon

Preparing a manuscript for submission to a publisher is simple. Always use standard white, 8.5-by-11-inch paper. Always choose to use Courier 10- or 12-point type, or as near as you can manage it, on one side of the paper. The text must be double-spaced. Always use left alignment, which creates ragged right margins. Margins should be set at one inch on all sides.

   Indent the first line of a paragraph by using the tab. Do not add an extra blank line between paragraphs. Although your computer and printer are capable of fancier layouts and fonts, do not be tempted to use them.

Never turn in a manuscript that is not page numbered. It is best to create a page header. The page header should identify the author, story, and page number on each page after the first, flush with the right page margin: Jones/Mississippi River Boats/2.

A manuscript is never stapled or bounded. Use paper clips only to hold the manuscript pages together. Be sure to use the correct size clip.

In the upper left corner of page 1, type the author's real name, address, phone number, and e-mail address. Also include an approximate word count, your tax ID or social security number, rights offered, and your copyright notice. You should round the word count to the nearest 10, 25, or 50 words. For example, if you have an article that is actually 917 words, it is OK to say the approximate word count is 920, 925, or 950.

You can also indicate if this is a "disposable copy"

if you only want the editor's reply but not the actual manuscript returned. (This saves on postage costs for you.)

When using your word processor, make sure the hyphenation setting is off.

Type the title and author's name (or pen name) centered about halfway down the first page. This is the byline that will be used when the work is published. The title should be in upper case.

Always remember that on the last page, you must include an indication that this is actually the end of the story: "###," "The End," or "—30—."

If you follow these simple rules, your manuscript will be properly formatted and acceptable to publishers. Sure you can use a Times Roman font, if you want, but you might submit to an editor that will not accept that font. It is always best to follow the rules to make sure you have prepared the manuscript properly.

—30—

Appendix B
Freelance Resources

As a freelancer, you can never be too rich, too thin, or have too much work. One of the ways to ensure plenty of opportunities is to have plenty of resources. Therefore, here is a wealth of sources for you to check out and use to develop your own resources based on your business model.

These many sources are your starting point. As you start your initial research, you will inevitably find other sources of information that will help your freelance career. Keep good notes and reference files. Because one of the problems of a freelancer is the pack rat syndrome, be sure to maintain your files so you can readily locate important resources when you need them.

Keep in mind that businesses and associations do tend to come and go, and change addresses, phone numbers, and web site addresses. Don't give up your search because a resource does not match precisely.

Writer Associations

American Crime Writers League, 18645 SW Farmington Road #255, Aloha, OR 97007.

American Society of Business Publication Editors, 710 E Ogden Avenue #600, Naperville IL 60563-8603, (630) 579-3288, Fax: (630)369-2488, e-mail: info@asbpe.org.

American Society of Journalists and Authors, 1501 Broadway #302, New York, NY 10036, (212) 997-0947, Fax: (212) 768-7414; www.asja.org.

Authors Guild, 31 East 28th Street, 10th Floor, New York, NY 10016, (212) 563-5904, www.authorsguild.org.

Beer Writers Guild, www.beerwritersguild.org.

Cat Writers Association, www.catwriters.org.

The Dog Writers Association of America, Inc. (DWAA), www.dwaa.org.

East Texas Writers' Guild, Catherine Sellers, President, P.O. Box 4597, Tyler, TX 75712, (903) 316-9431, e-mail: etwg@hotmail.com.

Editorial Freelancers Association, New York, NY, (212) 929-5400, Fax: (212) 929-5439, www.the-efa.org.

Florida Writers Association, 1345 E. Scots Avenue, Merritt Island, FL 32952, (321) 455-2986.

Garden Writers Association of America, 10210 Leatherleaf Court, Manassas, VA 20111, (703) 257-1032, Fax: 703-257-0213, www.gwaa.org.

Georgia Writers Association, English Department #2701, Kennesaw State University, 1000 Chastain Road, Kennesaw GA 30144, (770) 420-4736.

Gulf Coast Writers Association, P.O. Box 6445, Gulfport, MS 39506, www.gcwriters.org.

Houston Writers League, P.O. Box 550726, Houston, TX 77255-0726, www.houston writersleague.org.

Idaho Writers League, P.O. Box 1113, Hayden, ID 83835, www.idahowritersleague.com.

International Association of Crime Writers, P.O. Box 8674, New York, NY 10116, (212) 243-8966.

International Women's Writing Guild, P.O. Box 810, Gracie Station, New York, NY 10028, (212) 737-7536, www.iwwg.org.

Midwest Writers, Department of Journalism, Ball State University, Muncie, IN 47306, (765) 282-1055, www.midwestwriters.org.

National Association of Science Writers, P.O. Box 890, Hedgesville, WV 25427, (304) 754-5077, www.nasw.org.

National Association of Women Writers, P.O. Box 183812, Arlington, TX 76096, (866) 821-5829.

National Conference of Editorial Writers, 3899 North Front Street, Harrisburg, PA 17110, (717) 703-3015.

National League of American Pen Women, 1300 17th Street NW, Washington, DC 20036, (202) 785-1997.

National Writers Association, 10940 S Park Road #508, Parker, CO 80134, (303) 841-0246, Fax: (303) 841-2607, www.nationalwriters.com.

National Writers Union, 113 University Place, 6th Floor, New York, NY 10003, (212) 254-0279, www.nwu.org.

Outdoor Writers Association of America, 121 Hickory Street #1, Missoula, MT 59801, (406) 728-7434, www.owaa.org.

Pacific Northwest Writers Association, P.O. Box 2016, Edmonds, WA 98020, (425) 673-2665, www.pnwa.org.

Pen American Center, 568 Broadway, New York, NY 10012, (212) 334-1660, www.pen.org.

Philadelphia Writers, 535 Fairview Road, Medford, NJ 08055, (215) 497-9445, www.pwcwriters.org.

Society of American Travel Writers, 1500 Sunday Drive #102, Raleigh, NC 27607, (919) 861-5586, www.satw.org.

Society of Children's Book Writers and Illustrators, 8271 Beverly Boulevard, Los Angeles, CA 90048, (323) 782-1010. www.scbwi.com.

Society of Environmental Journalists, P.O. Box 2492, Jenkintown, PA 19046, (215) 884-8174, www.sej.org.

Society of Professional Journalists, 3909 North Meridian Street, Indianapolis, IN 46208, (317) 927-8000, www.spj.org.

Society of Southwestern Authors, P.O. Box 30355, Tucson, AZ 85751, (520) 546-9382, Fax: (520) 296-0409.

Books
Market Guides

American Book Trade Directory. Extensive directory that includes nearly 25,500 retail and antiquarian book dealers, plus 1,200 book and magazine wholesalers, distributors, and jobbers.

American Library Directory, two volumes. Includes detailed profiles for more than 37,000 public, academic, special, and government libraries and library-related organizations in the United States and Canada.

Directory of Editors, 32nd Edition (Paradise, CA: Dustbooks, 2001). Guide to the small press and magazine industry.

Herman, Jeff, *Jeff Herman's Guide to Book Publishers, Editors, and Literary Agents: 2007* (Waukesha, WI: Kalmbach Publishing, 2007). Extensive market guide for book authors.

International Literary Market Place 2007. Features 10,800 international book publishers and literary agents as well as 1,200 major booksellers and book clubs and 1,500 libraries.

Literary Market Place 2007, two volumes. The directory of the American book publishing industry, featuring 14,500 listings of publishers, printers, suppliers, and more.

The Writer's Handbook 2007 (Waukesha, WI: Kalmbach Publishing, 2007). Extensive market listings for book publishers, newspapers, magazines, and others that buy freelance writing.

Writer's Market (published annually by Writer's Digest Books, F+W Publications). Extensive market listings for book publishers, newspapers, magazines, and others that buy freelance writing. Online version also available.

Writing Books

Crawford, Tad, and Tony Lyons, *The Writer's Legal Guide* (New York: Allworth Press, 1996).

Herman, Jeff, and Deborah M. Adams, *Write the Perfect Book Proposal* (New York: John Wiley & Sons, 1993).

Levinson, Jay Conrad; Rick Frishman and Jill Lublin, *Guerilla Publicity* (Avon, MA: Adams Media, 2002).

Levinson, Jay Conrad; Rick Frishman and Michael Larson, *Guerilla Marketing for Writers* (Cincinnati, OH: Writer's Digest Books, 2000).

Specialized Writing Books

Burgett, Gordon, *Publishing to Niche Markets* (Santa Maria, CA: Communications Unlimited, 1995).

Burgett, Gordon, *Self-Publishing to Tightly-Targeted Markets* (Santa Maria, CA: Communications Unlimited, 1989).

Deval, Jacqueline, *Publicize Your Book! An Insider's Guide to Getting Your Book the Attention It Deserves* (New York: Perigee, 2003).

Eyman, Carol Luers, *How to Publish Your Newsletter: A Complete Guide to Print and Electronic Newsletter Publishing* (Garden City, NY: Square One).

Poynter, Dan, *Successful Nonfiction* (Santa Barbara, CA: Para Publishing, 2000).

Reference Books

Crawford, Tad, *Business and Legal Forms for Authors and Self-Publishers, Revised Edition* (New York: Allworth Press, 2000), with CD-ROM. Includes literary agent contracts, book publishing contracts, licensing contracts, privacy release, permission form, plus contracts with printers, sales reps, and distributors.

Poynter, Dan, *The Self-Publishing Manual, 14th Edition* (Santa Barbara, CA: Para Publishing, 2003).

General Resources

Media Finder, www.mediafinder.com.

Freelance Success, www.freelancesuccess.com.

MediaBistro, www.mediabistro.com.

Dice, www.dice.com.

CraigsList, www.craigslist.org.

Journalism Jobs, www.journalismjobs.com.

Online Resources

U.S. copyright law, www.copyright.gov.

Writers Conferences and Workshops, Shaw Guides, http://writing.shawguides.com.

Google Alert, www.googlealert.com (find references to your name, your books, etc. on the web).

Copyscape, www.copyscape.com (helps you determine if your web site pages have been copied).

Library of Congress, www.loc.gov.

International Standard Book Number Agency, www.isbn.org.

Editors and Preditors (lists of literary agents and other writers' services, with contact information, warnings about scams, etc.), http://anotherealm.com/prededitors.

www.DirPedia.com, (combining a dictionary, an encyclopedia, and a web directory).

Desk Reference, www.refdesk.com.

Efax Service, www.efax.com.

Telephone Answering Service, www.ringcentral.com.

Media Finder, www.mediafinder.com.

Magazines

Writer's Digest, www.writersdigest.com.

The Writer, www.writermag.com.

Writers Journal, www.writersjournal.com.

Software

Adobe, www.adobe.com.

Intuit (QuickBooks), www.quickbooks.com.

Microsoft (Office, Word, Excel), www.microsoft.com.

Consumable Suppliers

Office Depot, www.officedepot.com.

OfficeMax, www.officemax.com.

Quill, www.quill.com.

Staples, www.staples.com.

Glossary

Acquisitions editor: An editor that acquires material for a publisher by selection and negotiation with a writer or the writer's agent.

Agent: See literary agent.

Cataloging in publication: A block of information included in the front of the book for librarians; it includes a book's shelf category.

CD/R: Compact Disc/Recordable is a compact disc that is a Write Once, Read Many optical medium.

Compatibility: the ability of computer files created on one computer to be used on another computer.

Contact Manager: Software that keeps track of persons, associates, and tasks. Often integrates a calendar.

Copyeditor: The editor that evaluates the manuscript and makes corrections and alterations to fix spelling and grammatical errors, and to make the writing clearer.

Copy: Text or written material, still in a manuscript.

Database: A structured collection of records or data that is stored in a computer system.

DBA: Doing business as, a legal designation of a sole proprietorship, e.g., *Mary Jones dba The Write Shop.*

Gigabyte: A unit of computer memory or storage, often called gigs; a gigabyte is one billion bytes.

Logo: An identifying symbol used by businesses or organizations to establish their identities.

Telemarketing: The use of the telephone to solicit new business to sell a product or service.

Resolution: The clarity of the finished printed product created by a computer printer, scanner, or monitor. It is measured in dpi (dots per inch).

Deadline: A time set to turn in material to an editor or publisher.

Bandwidth: A metaphorical description of the amount of data that can be transferred to or from the web site or server, measured in bytes transferred over a prescribed period.

Chat room: A method of communicating by sending real time text messages among computer users with similar interests.

Executive editor: An editor that is involved with management rather than editing or writing material.

First North American Serial Rights (FNASR): The exclusive right to publish material in a newspaper, magazine, or newsletter within North America for the first time.

Flat rate: Work done for a fee, regardless of the number of hours it takes to complete the work.

Folio: The page number.

Font: The type style.

Freelancer: A self-employed person who works on a project or contact basis to produce a manuscript or artwork.

Front matter: All pages before the main body of the text (in a book, it is the title page, table of contents, acknowledgments, foreword, etc.).

Galley: Page proofs from a commercial printer.

Ghostwriter: Someone that writes for another and receives money, but no credit, for the work; someone else takes credit for the work.

Gutter: Interior margin of the book that is bound.

HTML: Hypertext Markup Language, the code used to assemble web site pages.

Imprint: The identifying name of a series of books from a publisher under a parent company.

International Standard Book Number (ISBN): A number assigned by publishers and used to identify a book by edition, binding, and publisher.

International Standard Serial Number (ISSN): A number assigned by the Library of Congress to identify serial publications.

Library of Congress (LOC): The national library of the United States and research arm of the United States Congress; located in Washington, DC.

Literary agent: A person that represents a writer and markets the writer's work to publishers; most only accept screenplays or books.

News release: A one- or two-page document designed to alert the media about a topic or subject, often called a "press release."

Nonfiction: An article or book that contains only the truth, and no fictional or made-up facts or stories.

Pantone Matching System (PMS): A registered trade name for a system of numbered ink colors.

PDF: The Portable Document Format is the computer file format created and controlled by Adobe Systems for document exchange.

Print on Demand (POD): The process of printing a book when it is ordered; each page is printed individually, rather than with a signature.

Production editor: The person that oversees a large project and makes certain all elements come together to meet a deadline.

Proofreader: The person that reviews typeset material, checking for accuracy and looking for errors.

Query: A letter suggesting or pitching an idea for an article or book. The letter is created by the writer and sent to an editor or agent.

Rejection: A formal turn-down from an editor to a writer over material submitted on speculation.

Retainer: An amount of money paid in advance for services.

Serial: Ongoing publication such as a magazine, newspaper, or newsletter.

Sidebar: A small article inserted in a publication that compliments the main text.

Signature: A large sheet of printed pages, which when folded and cut, become a part of a book or publication.

Spam: Unwanted and unsolicited e-mail sent to large numbers of uninterested computer users.

Speculation: The submission of a manuscript without the guarantee of acceptance.

Uniform Resource Locator (URL): An internet address used to find a web site.

WFH: See *work for hire*.

Word processor: A person that creates text documents using computer software or a software program that allows users to type text into a computer and format it.

Work for hire: Material produced under a written agreement by a freelancer where by all rights have been assigned to the publisher.

Index